AF477163

Book of Enoch

The Ways of God, Angels, and Men

by

Anders Bennett

ADISAN Publishing AB

Most, if not all, quotes in the Book of Enoch writing project are sourced from:

- **R.H. Charles - The Book of Enoch (1917)**

- **R. Laurence - The Book of Enoch (1883)**

That are available in Public Domain for reference. With other sources used for comprehension or further research on concepts. These are mentioned in the Bibliography section of the book.

*"Enoch walked with God;
then he was no more,
because God took him."*
Genesis 5:24

CONTENTS

* numbers in Brackets belong to book by R.H. Charles - The Book of Enoch (1917)

Where is the Book of Enoch Now?

The Book of Enoch has enjoyed more than three popular translations since the discovery of the Ethiopic text in 1773 by Scottish explorer James Bruce. Traveling to far away Ethiopia, Bruce discovered the Book of Enoch faithfully preserved by the Ethiopian Orthodox church, placing the text right alongside the other books of their Bible.

Having secured not one but three Ethiopian copies of the book, Bruce brought them back to Britain. Richard Laurence then published the very first English translation in 1821. While the more popular edition by R.H. Charles was published in 1912.

While not as well-known as other religious texts in publication, The Book of Enoch deserves to be as popular as the recent translations of Gnostic works made available from the latest discoveries like the *Gospel of Judas*. or the centuries-old apocryphal resource on the lives of the Saints by Jacobus Voragine called the *Golden Legend*; for the obvious influence it has over the origin stories with relation to the "children of God" also known as Angels.

The Book of Enoch has had many translations that have been very academic in nature, often daunting and inaccessible to the modern reader. Some readers do not prefer being overwhelmed by a book. They prefer to maintain interest in a topic with a style and language they can relate to with references and authoritative sources that add to their knowledge and not burden them as they read.

Angels and Demons have occupied a special place in the human imagination. All across cultures, there are beings of light and monsters from the dark. They personify the continued struggle between two opposing forces: light and darkness, Heaven and Hell, good and evil. A struggle that is still considered by many as ongoing even in the secular world.

Roman Catholics are familiar with statues and paintings of Michael the Archangel stepping on the body of Lucifer while brandishing a flaming sword. Christians know of the Nativity story that began with Angel Gabriel's Annunciation to the Virgin Mary to the choir of angels that heralded the birth of the Messiah to the shepherds out in the fields.

Even Lucifer has evolved from Heaven's adversary to a detective's consultant on television. But no other two beings occupy the top spot in popular culture as angels and demons do.

To give the reader a sense of wonder as he goes through the pages of the book, we shall provide them with easily understandable notes from the references, either short blurbs or excursus, to enhance their reading experience. Names will be given meanings, symbols and iconographies will be explored from source to current evolved forms, themes from myth, legend, and lore will be cross-referenced, and their relevance will be discussed.

The book shall have no pretensions to highbrow academic scholarship but will seek to be properly researched, helpful, and prove itself reliable to readers.

INTRODUCTION

The power of a single word is remarkable. Letters put together, each with specific sounds creating a single unit of speech, identify people, places, and objects. Given particular meaning, they can represent simple to sophisticated action, even abstract concepts that can give identity, express desire, stress disgust, call people to action, and even change the world.

Take, for example, the word *God* with the capital 'G' in the Judeo - Christian context refers to the all-powerful and all-knowing being who is *"Lord of all creation"* and is the beginning [Alpha] and end [Omega] of everything we know. But change the first letter with a smaller 'g' to *god*, then what you have is a deity who exists with others of his kind, has control over a particular element of nature [*Zeus*, the Greek god of thunder], a universally felt or known concept [*Venus*, the Roman goddess of love], or an aspect of the cycle of existence [*Shiva*, Hindu god of destruction]; all with specific powers but possessing very human qualities and failings that they most often change or affect the course of humanity because they end up squabbling amongst themselves.

Words put together are the seeds of ideas. And ever since man first attempted to explain the workings of the world around him, from the rising and setting of the sun, the changing of the seasons, to the fruits of the earth, science was not the first option.

Our first explanations of the workings of the universe were supernatural. The idea that a greater being was responsible for our existence is as old as the human race itself. When words moved from being spoken to being written, they were given the power to endure not only as text but as solidified ideas that would develop into songs, myths, legends, epics, histories, theologies, philosophies, and eventually into modern scientific thought.

Consider then these thirteen words from Chapter 5, verse 24 from the Book of Genesis:

"Enoch walked with God;
then he was no more,
because God took him."

For the unfamiliar reader, Enoch is a character in the Old Testament of the Bible, mentioned in passing under the genealogy of Adam, for living three hundred and sixty-five years and for fathering Methuselah, the grandfather of Noah [Genesis 5:22-23], who later on, would build the Ark as instructed by God in anticipation of the Great Flood.

Yet somehow, these thirteen words held such power over the imagination of the ancient Hebrews from long ago that Enoch became the key character in his own book. In these modern times, The Book of Enoch is what we consider a "spin-off" of the Genesis story; a supplemental or forgotten chapter perhaps from the early days of mankind that affected our very view of the workings of heaven and earth much like it does when beloved side characters are given their own back story of separate plot in comic books, movies, or television series.

Enoch was a man, no different from his forefathers too, but there was something special about him. When they said *"Ambulavitque cum Deo"* [Enoch walked with God] in Genesis 5:24. Those words traditionally meant that Enoch was, by their standards, a good man, a man of strong faith, a man who never faltered and was obedient to God's will. Even Jesus Christ, in his teachings centuries after, invites his followers to *"walk with him"* as read in the Gospels.

In the Latin Vulgate, Genesis 5:17 says, *"et facti sunt omnes dies Malalehel octingenti nonaginta quinque anni et mortuus est"*; which is translated to "And all the days of Malalehel were eight hundred and ninety-five years, and he died."

The same was said for Enoch's father, Jared, in Genesis 5:20. *"Et facti sunt omnes dies Iared nongenti sexaginta duo anni et mortuus est"* is also worded somewhat the same as before and translated thus: "And all the days of Jared were nine hundred and sixty-two years, and he died." But when we get to Enoch, the Latin Vulgate was clear on this:

"... Et non apparuit quia tulit eum Deus."
[... And was seen no more: because God took him.]

Notice the difference between Enoch's father and his grandfather? While Genesis 5:17 and 5:20 were clear on the deaths, *"et mortus est"* [and he died], of Jared and Malaleel, it definitely differentiates Enoch for having been taken by God.

So where did God take Enoch, you might ask?

That is where this book will take you. Enoch was introduced to the "children of God," became witness to highly fantastical visions, traveled the realms of what was created, and saw a war that shook the very foundations of heaven and earth; expanding from another verse in Genesis that spoke of ill times when giants walked the earth.

The primary text which this book will be referring to is the Ethiopic Book of Enoch as translated by George Henry Schodde [1854-1917]. Scholars agree that the First Book of Enoch was originally Aramaic in origin, seen as authentic and inspired by certain Jewish sects around the first century B.C.E., gaining popularity for five more centuries.

Apocalyptic in nature, studies have also yielded that there is no singular Book of Enoch, but rather it is an amalgam of several manuscripts penned by different authors, possibly at different time periods. Some have even ascribed sections to Enoch and Noah. The Ethiopian text, by far, is considered the most extensive and diverse of all three, the two others being the Slavonic and the Hebraic Books of Enoch.

The Ethiopian text that was translated by George Henry Schodde was said to have been derived from a Greek manuscript that was assumed also to be a copy of an older text. Discovered in the 18th century, The First Book of Enoch was initially dated to have been penned during the early years of Christianity, seen as having quoted content that was assumed to have been drawn and paraphrased from the New Testament.

Another theory, however, rooted in the recent discoveries of copies of the Book of Enoch with the Dead Sea Scrolls at Qumran, claims the book existed way before Jesus Christ's time, estimated at two centuries. Thus, it can be assumed that the Book of Enoch may have been quoted by and influenced the writers of the New Testament and may have influenced the teachings of Jesus himself.

The Book of Enoch, while not entirely seen as purely authentic by the first Christians, they felt that its contents were inspired and worthy of belief. From the existence of angels, the order of the cosmos as they understood it, to the origins of evil upon this earth.

As we move from chapter to chapter, we shall study the themes found in the visions as witnessed by Enoch, the ancient struggles in heaven and earth, delve into commentary with regards to the iconography and symbolism and illustrate the parallels between the Biblical texts and those found in the Book of Enoch, and how these resonated and evolved through millennia, finding themselves relevant into our current Christian zeitgeist.

Our journey with Enoch within these pages will familiarize us with a book that is not widely known to the modern reader but was surely influential in the development of Christian Theology as we are familiar with it today.

Let us now walk with Enoch, who once walked with God and showed us things though beyond belief, endures with us still.

CHAPTER ONE:

THE BOOK OF THE WATCHERS

[Enoch 1 – 36]

Chapter One:

The Book of the Watchers

The first chapter or part in the Book of Enoch begins with Enoch's vision on Mount Sinai provided by the angels who loyally followed God. Out of context, it might be odd to refer to these angels as loyal, as the generalization with all angels in our modern times is that they all are loyal to God's word. Unfortunately, this is not always the case. As the Book of Enoch will reveal later, some angels created by the Lord would fall both figuratively in their values and even literally as they descended down to earth to reside next to the man. For Enoch's tale this is shown prominently through the Watchers. The Watchers are described as angels with a specific purpose for their creation; to watch or oversee all that is occurring on the earth, including the activities of man and animals alike. Simply put, their designated job is to observe, hence their name. As Enoch journeys into the residence of God, he will begin to learn the secrets of the Watchers, Archangels, and celestial beasts that reside and work in heaven.

Throughout the book of Enoch, it is not detailed exactly as to why Enoch was chosen to receive these visions and opportunities he did. From what we know about Enoch, he seemed to live an average life for the most part of his time on earth, assumingly in a modest and humble fashion. One area where Enoch would be found extraordinary is from his direct bloodline to Adam, the first man created. Although roughly a seven generational gap was between them, it was apparent through time and action that Enoch and his family were loyal followers of God. With these words of blessing, Enoch had begun to clearly understand what was being shown as not only occurrences that would affect his own generation through the actions the watchers had taken, but as a vision that would affect a future generation that has yet to come. With this prediction, Enoch recalls it as a great event where God, or The Holy Great One as He is occasionally referred to in the Book of Enoch, will come forth to Earth with all the strength and might of what is present in the heavens. According to Enoch, this event will bring along a great instance of what many would believe as a 'judgment day' among all human beings across the world.

To give more context on what struggles the world was facing in the time of Enoch, it is important to note what had occurred in order for these conflicts to emerge. Ever since the days of Adam, there has been a temptation in the form of rebelling against the Lord's will in both man and angelic beings alike. Just as the well-known story of the angel Lucifer straying from God's ideals and emerging to tempt Adam and Eve into corruption eventually, Enoch will soon recall the instances and complexities that this and additional fallen angels who followed in Lucifer's path would soon entail.

As the first angel had fallen, five others had soon followed down to earth. Although in these times, it wasn't uncommon for angels to communicate more fluidly and openly with humans, this instance of Watchers leaving their post was not in good faith.

From what was understood by Enoch, these Watchers had continuously overseen all that humans were privileged to do, including creating their own offspring and families for generations. Seeing this and being coerced by wickedness itself in the form of Lucifer, the Watchers decided to attempt something never done by angels of their kind before; descend to the earth and live as humans do. Optimistically, this plan might have the chance to become beneficial, but just as people can become swayed into corruption in our modern times, whether in their personal or professional life, the Watchers had taken advantage of their situation and began testing their boundaries through their human-esque lifestyles.

As the Watchers began fraternizing with humans, they eventually became successful in birthing their own offspring, which in many ways was a significant step in the increasing corruption of earth and humanity. These offspring of half-angel and human were deemed the Nephilim; described as huge giants; their very being as a mix of celestial and terrestrial beings made them unstable and prone to chaos.

To make matters worse, the influence of the fallen angels upon the Nephilim encouraged destruction and violence, as it was noted that some of the fallen had gained pleasure in teaching both Nephilim and humans the ways to create various weapons made of metals. From swords and daggers to shields and breastplates, this may be the first notable incident of crafting items that are harmless in themselves, but with the encouragement and individualistic approach to living from the Watchers, their use quickly became associated with ill-minded actions such as battles, disagreement, and war.

In addition to weaponry, materialism quickly gained hold of those on earth as well in the form of decoration. Objects such as jewelry and ornaments were crafted quickly with ideals of desiring material objects and finding worth in them over the meaning of faith or the wellbeing of their fellow man. Although these objects in themselves are not technically 'bad' in their own right, the concepts of their importance overtook humans, making the word of God seem as more of a suggestion without importance, and had begun an era of negative thinking, corruption, and individualism to the point of causing harm to others. For perspective, this new era of corruption brought on by the watchers is comparable to what we see in our modern world today.

Corruption and temptation of material things are spiritually frowned upon, but in the age of social media and consumerism, our societies are influenced by a plethora of content promoting extravagance, leading to the conclusion that in order to become successful or deemed worthy, one must own more possessions than they could count. Images of expense show how a person should be received instead of their character and actions. As one may notice, going down this path of life and living for objects instead of using said objects to live can easily lead to a habit of poor quality of life and lack of fulfillment in one's personal goals, making it important to keep moderation in mind as the truth shows wealth in a less than luxurious light.

And all shall be smitten with fear
And the Watchers shall quake,
And great fear and trembling shall seize them unto the ends of the earth.
And the high mountains shall be shaken,
And the high hills shall be made low,
And shall melt like wax before the flame
And the earth shall be wholly rent in sunder,
And all that is upon the earth shall perish,
And there shall be a judgement upon all (men)."

At first glance, this event may seem catastrophic and may lead to feelings of fear, but in reality, this is not the case. As many scriptures from this book and others mention, God is a forgiving and righteous figure who acts with purpose. Reading further, one could think of this event as more of a 'reset' to help rid the world of corruption and wrongdoing forces that may cause people to stray from what is good and truthful.

Another parallel this could be foreshadowing in Biblical stories is the instance of the Great Flood (which will be covered in part by the Book of Enoch later on in this work). When God eventually determined the corruption of the world became too strong in its negative influences, He called for a 'reset' to transform the world for the better. Similarly, in nature, an ecosystem can flourish for decades, but if an aggressively invasive species finds its way in, the unchecked plant or animal can wreak havoc on native populations and throw off the balance of a fragile environment. In this case, as the problem continues to smother and conquer what was before it, one might need to call upon outside help to re-balance the environment.

"But with the righteous He will make peace.
And will protect the elect,
And mercy shall be upon them.
And they shall all belong to God,
And they shall be prospered,
And they shall all be blessed.
And He will help them all,
And light shall appear unto them,
And He will make peace with them'.
And behold! He cometh with ten thousand of His holy ones
To execute judgement upon all,
And to destroy all the ungodly:
And to convict all flesh
Of all the works of their ungodliness which they have ungodly committed,
And of all the hard things which ungodly sinners have spoken against Him."

As Enoch learned more, he noticed that this prediction has a positive and a beneficial means to an end. This understanding is further explained as observations of continuous change and consistency are shown throughout nature, from the stars and luminaries following the same orbits for centuries to the changing of the seasons that the entire planet goes through. From the cold frigid months of winter to the emergence of flower blossoms and warmer weather in the spring and summer, these natural occurrences follow their patterns of change steadily and without worry.

Imagine a time when change was inevitable in life. Changing schools, starting a new job, and even moving to a new place to live are all instances of change that many of us will eventually go through in life at some point. As one may already know, these changes might not be scary to think about on their own, but the anticipation of going through change can cause nerves to skyrocket. Thinking of "what-ifs" can be polarizing on its own, but when the time can be found to slow down these anxieties, the situation isn't as bad as it might appear to be. For many, there is no true way to predict the future on if a new school or workplace will be the perfect fit, but instead of accuracy in what is to come, there is hope and faith; hope and faith in oneself, faith in a positive outcome of fate, and the idea that what is guiding us will be beneficial and true. In the end, finding what is right and maintaining the perseverance to continue to reach that goal is what can not only help us adapt to changes and the unknown but can strengthen our faith as a whole.

Faith can be found in everyday life as well when faced with any uncertainties. When the sun begins to fall, we have faith that it will rise again to start another day. When the summer starts to cool, and plants begin to be covered by icy blankets of snow, there is faith that they will rebloom next season. In Enoch's case, this faith is tied to the idea that while the pain of corruption acted upon by others affects the innocent, there will be time to reconcile those who caused harm and bless those who are most deserving with a refreshed life.

"And for all of you sinners there shall be no salvation,
But on you all shall abide a curse.
But for the elect there shall be light and joy and peace,
And they shall inherit the earth."

Before this vision experienced by Enoch was to become fulfilled, the first major catastrophic event would occur; the creation of offspring between angels and humans. After admiring the beauty of the daughters of humanity from afar, many angels chose to descend to the earth in order to make them their wives and have them bear their children. As the fallen angels decided to carry out their new goal Azazel, a fellow former angel, continued working on supporting this agenda of disaster by teaching the new generation of humanity new methods of creating weaponry to add to the chaos. According to Enoch's depictions, Azazel had taught humans the way of creating items such as swords, knives, shields, and armor with the natural metals of the earth.

"And Azazel taught men to make swords, and knives, and shields, and breastplates, and made known to them the metals of the earth and the art of working them, and bracelets, and ornaments, and the use of antimony, and the beautifying of the eyelids, and all kinds of costly stones, and all[2] colouring tinctures. And there arose much godlessness, and they committed fornication, and they[3] were led astray, and became corrupt in all their ways."

As this continued, the angels above in the heavens heard the cries and struggles from down on earth and carried the message to God in order to repair the chaos the fallen had created.

"Go to Noah and tell him in my name 'Hide thyself!' and reveal to him the end that is approaching: that the whole earth will be destroyed, and a deluge is about to come[3] upon the whole earth and will destroy all that is on it. And now instruct him that he may escape[4], and his seed may be preserved for all the generations of the world."

Enoch's tale now moves forward toward the preparation of Noah's Ark and the Great Flood. To pay for his betrayal, Azazel the fallen angel was further bound and cast into the darkness with any other Watchers that had participated in creating their own offspring with humans and designated to become judged for their wrongdoings once the day of judgment had arrived. By doing so, this would re-balance the earth towards peace, harmony, and the well-being of those who lived upon it.

As the Watchers were reprimanded for their actions, the remaining angels loyal to the guidance of God began to wage their fight against the children of the Watchers, who were known to be aggressive giants, bringing havoc and endangering the rest of mankind. With the wisdom of God through hearing His voice, Enoch had learned of all the intentions that were brought on by these giants, what was to come in order to bring harmony to the world, and of the sparing of true believers who were righteous in their intentions.

"And now, the giants, who are produced from the spirits and flesh, shall be called evil spirits upon[9] the earth, and on the earth shall be their dwelling. Evil spirits have proceeded from their bodies; because they are born from men and from the holy Watchers is their beginning and primal origin;[10] they shall be evil spirits on earth, and evil spirits shall they be called. [As for the spirits of heaven, in heaven shall be their dwelling, but as for the spirits of the earth which were born upon the earth, on the earth shall be their dwelling.] And the spirits of the giants afflict, oppress, destroy, attack, do battle, and work destruction on the earth, and cause trouble: they take no food, but nevertheless[12] hunger and thirst, and cause offenses."

Following these instructions, Enoch had experienced another version of what punishment awaited the Watchers. in contradiction to heaven or Earth; this envisioned place was described only as chaotic and horrible. A place nearly unimaginable but was the very essence of fear and pain, as it was created to imprison angels who had turned into darkness. As Enoch's visions continued, the angel Raphael who was guiding him, carried him towards another deep and dark hollow where human spirits who had done their wrongdoings in life would arrive at their final destination.

With these descriptions, one might think of our modern imagery of Hell or Tartarus. A place where darkness and emptiness only reside, or in the case of the corrupt watchers, a place where unrest and struggling would overcome their wrongdoings on earth. According to Enoch, these two distinct areas where human and angelic spirits would be collected are similar in some ways, but due to their differences in abilities and former strengths, the consequences for their actions may increase in intensity.

Similar to how Enoch was able to gain a preview of the inner workings of where negatively judged spirits would find the end of their journey, there was also light and beauty on its polar opposite. Towards the end of his visions in this first chapter, Enoch finally alludes to viewing several earth-like destinations filled with beasts, birds, and plant life that was prolific and abundant, fully blessed to its best potential. As with many changes and cycles found within our physical earth, Enoch has shown that there are two options within the Lord's judgment; a dark, dank emptiness or a flourishing, diverse, and blessed environment.

"And from thence I went to the south to the ends of the earth, and saw there three open portals [2] of the heaven: and thence there come dew, rain, and wind. And from thence I went to the east to the ends of the heaven, and saw here the three eastern portals of heaven open and small portals [3] above them. Through each of these small portals pass the stars of heaven and run their course to the west on the path which is shown to them. And as often as I saw I blessed always the Lord of Glory, and I continued to bless the Lord of Glory who has wrought great and glorious wonders, to show the greatness

of His work to the angels and to spirits and to men, that they might praise His work and all His creation: that they might see the work of His might and praise the great work of His hands and bless Him forever."

Overall, as Enoch begins his blessings in understanding and receiving visions of the heavens from the Lord, there are already many lessons to be learned. The fall of the Watchers, who are defined as corrupt angelic beings, is a surprising event to those who may not have heard of the event before. As angelic beings, the general census defines them as pure followers of God, so how could even they fall? As Enoch discovers, the answers lie in corruption and temptation. Just as Adam and Eve were tempted from the perspective of humans, the same can apply to the Watchers' situation. As they began, the Watchers' duties involved descending from heaven to walk and observe humans on earth or 'watch' them as they go along their lives. The general census of their permissions also included the Watchers being granted special authority to speak in place and as a representative of God. In general, this meant that they even had the permission to interfere in human affairs, if necessary, at times as well, and only with the intentions aligned with the Lord.

As time carried on, one of the Watchers' leaders began to fraternize more and more with humans in a near-problematic way. The life cycles of people on Earth were observed often, from birth to finding a life partner and carrying on the cycle of one's lineage. Eventually, through seeing this, the temptation for some of the watchers emerged. As they realized their desire to live as humans, their plan began to involve taking their own wives as well in order to carry on their own characteristics into the next generation, which would soon become their own downfall as they had abused their authorizations and brought conflict and chaos into the world through the emergence of their offspring, the Nephilim.

CHAPTER TWO:

THE BOOK OF THE PARABLES

[Enoch 37 – 71]

Chapter Two:

The Book of the Parables

After Enoch had experienced his first vision of what consequences were in store after the defiling and disobedient acts that the Watchers had caused, a second vision would soon be manifested through a series of parables or lessons meant to explain a critical moral situation. Similar to the tales Jesus would eventually spread across the Holy Land, Enoch received his second vision of wisdom and understanding of three parables that were given to him through the words of the Lord that he heard. As Enoch began to understand the meaning behind these parables, it was evident that they were to act as present and future guidelines towards keeping one's actions in line with the righteous goodness of the will of God.

Additionally, at this time, Enoch had begun to learn of the privilege he had in the opportunity to eventually share the parables that he had learned of with his descendants. Content-wise, Enoch's parables taught similar morals to the tellings of Jesus documented later on in the New Testament, but with one major contrasting detail in their audience base. In Enoch's case, the parables he envisioned and spoke of were seemingly directed towards his immediate family, although they were eventually documented and published for all to understand, hence the opportunities for us to study them even in modern times.

On the other side of the spectrum, the parables taught by Jesus were directed to hundreds of his followers at the time of their tellings and again were eventually recorded and passed down in order to keep them viable even today.

"When the congregation of the righteous shall appear,
And sinners shall be judged for their sins,
And shall be driven from the face of the earth:
² And when the Righteous One shall appear before the eyes of the righteous,
Whose elect works hang upon the Lord of Spirits,
And light shall appear to the righteous and the elect who dwell on the earth,
Where then will be the dwelling of the sinners,
And where the resting-place of those who have denied the Lord of Spirits?
It had been good for them if they had not been born.
³ When the secrets of the righteous shall be revealed and the sinners judged,
And the godless driven from the presence of the righteous and elect,
⁴ From that time those that possess the earth shall no longer be powerful
*   and exalted:*
And they shall not be able to behold the face of the holy,
For the Lord of Spirits has caused His light to appear
On the face of the holy, righteous, and elect.
⁵ Then shall the kings and the mighty perish
And be given into the hands of the righteous and holy.
⁶ And thenceforward none shall seek for themselves mercy from the
*   Lord of Spirits*
For their life is at an end."

In this first parable, Enoch hears the message of justice being cast upon the world or the eventual coming of judgment day for the wicked-on earth. With this information, Enoch learns that as they are judged, they will be quickly removed from the earth and towards their designated resting place. To emphasize the importance of this incident for all who were accused wrongly in the eyes of the Lords and turned wicked in their ways, Enoch reveals that during this process of judgment and decision-making, there will be a time when any power and authority held in the sinners' hands would be stripped away.

As the first book of the Watchers describes, in the time of Enoch, there was eventually a lot of corruption on the earth by both humans and angels alike, with the latter taking advantage of the former for personal interests through creating giants and immersing themselves in human activities. Resulting from this corruption, Enoch had understood that a great change would be needed and had been foretold to occur from God to bring the righteous their peace and the wrongdoers their punishment.

In our time, it is easy to see similarities between our own societies and Enoch's experience in the challenges his own community faced. Today, there are those who continue to stray from the guidelines and rules set by God in the form of committing crimes, harming others, or being deceitful in their intentions. As Enoch later noted, with the removal of power from the sinners, the implication that judgment will be carried out fairly among those who may hold more prestigious titles than their peers.

This idea is continued to be reinforced, as Enoch's vision distinguishes that even the kings and mighty would not be able to use their power or influence to give them an advantage over the consequences of their actions. In fact, the very opposite would occur, as those who were judged to be righteous would then uptake these leadership responsibilities.

Imagine teaming up to complete a work project with a lackluster coworker, reluctant to work. Although they aren't willing to contribute equally, there is a high chance that they will still try to claim ownership of the project. Adding in the potential for a raise or reward by the boss, these chances skyrocket. Is it justifiable for that coworker to receive the same benefits as another who was genuine? Of course not, and logically an observant employer would notice these patterns in behavior to put a stop to them as soon as possible. Fortunately, as soon as God had seen and heard of the ill-intentions of the Watchers and their results from the disobedience and chaos, He had already begun to craft a plan on how to ensure those who acted wrongly faced their appropriate justice while the innocent were given a new opportunity for flourishing. Likewise, many Archangels who remained loyal in their sidings with

God decided to plead towards Him, asking for redemption for the actions of His beloved-created humans, as many of them were persuaded and affected by the Watchers' action and the world they influenced. Naturally, God heard these pleas and cries for mercy with a new beginning and was determined to improve the entire situation in a way that only He could. In the case of the workplace metaphor, the Lord was the most observant and actionable leader, ready to create and carry out a foolproof plan that began with Enoch's journey and ended in the judgment of all Nephilim and Watchers on earth through cleansing it and beginning anew. As the most observant boss, it is clear that these former coworkers were to be stopped promptly.

"And after that I saw thousands of thousands and ten thousand times ten thousand, I saw a multitude [2] beyond number and reckoning, who stood before the Lord of Spirits. And on the four sides of the Lord of Spirits I saw four presences, different from those that sleep not, and I learnt their names: for the angel that went with me made known to me their names, and showed me all the hidden things. [3] And I heard the voices of those four presences as they uttered praises before the Lord of glory."

As Enoch notices further through his vision, he then experiences encountering the four angels of the Lord of Spirits; Michael, Raphael, Gabriel, and Phanuel. Enoch hears these four archangels speaking praises in the name of the Lord, including blessing the Lord of Spirits while interceding any dark souls or corruptors from preventing others from coming to the Lord. *(In the book of Enoch, there are many names used for God, including the Lord of Glory, Lord of Spirits, or the Holy One. As all refer to the divine nature of God themselves, they are used across the scriptures interchangeably).*

Following the previous visions Enoch had received from the Lord, not to mention the words heard by the Archangels doing their work to bring redemption to as many as they could, the hierarchies of the heavens and the weight of man's actions had become clear.

"And they give thanks and praise and rest not;
For unto them is their thanksgiving rest.

For the sun changes oft for a blessing or a curse,
And the course of the path of the moon is light to the righteous
And darkness to the sinners in the name of the Lord,
Who made a separation between the light and the darkness,
And divided the spirits of men,
And strengthened the spirits of the righteous,
In the name of His righteousness.

⁹ For no angel hinders and no power is able to hinder; for He appoints a judge for them all and He judges them all before Him."

At this point, Enoch had fully understood that regardless of the status one may have as an angel or human, the Lord is still capable and willing to enact the appropriate justice upon any wrongdoers. Following this understanding, Enoch had next had their second parable, further revealing the dwelling of the angels and Lord. Naturally, this area would further be understood as sacred and as a place where no evil-doer or sinner would be able to set foot.

"And there I saw One who had a head of days,
And His head was white like wool,
And with Him was another being whose countenance had the appearance
*   of a man,*
And his face was full of graciousness, like one of the holy angels.
² And I asked the angel who went with me and showed me all the hidden
*   things, concerning that*
³ Son of Man, who he was, and whence he was, (and) why he went with
*   the Head of Days? And he answered and said unto me:*
This is the son of Man who hath righteousness,
With whom dwelleth righteousness,
And who revealeth all the treasures of that which is hidden,
Because the Lord of Spirits hath chosen him,
And whose lot hath the pre-eminence before the Lord of Spirits in
*   uprightness for ever."*

Regarding this next statement by Enoch, another extraordinary envisionment had occurred, this time in the form of the Lord with a future premonition of the Son of Man. After learning of the existence of the

Son of Man, Enoch realized the importance that was still to be as this Son will raise the strongest kings from their thrones, and influence many, true and sinful, to result in a congregation of faithful and honest followers. As it may sound already, this is a distinct premonition of the comings and actions of Jesus, who was destined to be an example and create a never-before-seen impact on the earth for hundreds of years.

Finally, the third parable of Enoch was to be understood. Through the third parable, Enoch learned of all the blessings that were to come for the true and righteous, as the blessings of light and peace would be bestowed upon them.

"And I began to speak the third Parable concerning the righteous and elect.
2 Blessed are ye, ye righteous and elect,
For glorious shall be your lot.
3 And the righteous shall be in the light of the sun.
And the elect in the light of eternal life:
The days of their life shall be unending,
And the days of the holy without number.
4 And they shall seek the light and find righteousness with the Lord of Spirits:
There shall be peace to the righteous in the name of the Eternal Lord.
5 And after this it shall be said to the holy in heaven
That they should seek out the secrets of righteousness, the heritage of faith:
For it has become bright as the sun upon earth,
And the darkness is past.
6 And there shall be a light that never endeth,
And to a limit (lit. ' number ') of days they shall not come,
For the darkness shall first have been destroyed,
[And the light established before the Lord of Spirits]
And the light of uprightness established for ever before the Lord of Spirits."

Like that of an observant and just employer, the Lord had promised to Enoch and all that were loyal and true that they would receive their blessings for their good work and perseverance. The people wouldn't go unnoticed, as He was always watching, and instead would be eternally graced with all that is good. Through Enoch's visions and parables, he witnessed the inner workings of the heavens were explained in a clear manner, but Enoch's journey into the tiers of heaven was still in continuation towards what was still to come.

After Enoch had experienced all of the inner workings and processes of judgment upon all who fell under the Lord, angel, and human alike, his grandson Noah would discover the time for this judgment and cleansing would be arriving. After experiencing a series of visions depicting the earth sinking into destruction, Noah had called aloud to his grandfather for guidance.

"…and Noah said three times with an embittered voice: Hear me, hear me, hear me.' And I said unto him: 'Tell me what it is that is falling out on the earth that the earth is in such evil plight [4] and shaken, lest perchance I shall perish with it? "

Responding, Enoch began to explain that due to the world's undoing through violence and misuse brought upon fallen angels, their judgment is inevitable and necessary to restore harmony and peace for the rest of the world. Unfortunately, at this point in time, this means that many of the areas that were tainted would need to be destroyed in the process.

To further explain this upcoming phenomenon, Enoch showed Noah all the preparations the angels had made to let loose the strength of the Earth's water to commence the era of judgment. From here, Noah was instructed to create a vessel that would be blessed by the Lord and shall protect all the innocent who lacked blame safely through these times of judgment. By doing so, Noah would allow the earth to reestablish itself after a flood of judgment had passed in order to reclaim the world for good. After Enoch had shared his own witness on what was to come for his grandson Noah, eventually, the time was set for Enoch himself to ascend to the heavens to rest and become with the Lord for eternity.

"And he (i.e. the angel) came to me and greeted me with His voice, and
    said unto me '
This is the Son of Man who is born unto righteousness,
And righteousness abides over him,
And the righteousness of the Head of Days forsakes him not.'

¹⁵ And he said unto me:
'He proclaims unto thee peace in the name of the world to come;
For from hence has proceeded peace since the creation of the world,
And so shall it be unto thee for ever and for ever and ever.
¹⁶ And all shall walk in his ways since righteousness never forsaketh him:
With him will be their dwelling-places, and with him their heritage,
And they shall not be separated from him for ever and ever and ever.
And so there shall be length of days with that Son of Man,
And the righteous shall have peace and an upright way
In the name of the Lord of Spirits for ever and ever."

In all, these parables are simply a preview into what Enoch's journey will teach him and the lessons he would later share with those
further in his lineage. One major theme that one should take away
from this second chapter of parables is the importance of unbiased
judgment, acted upon in the Lord's guidance. One common way to
imagine the processes of the Lord's judgement is through the process
of modern-day law and order on a state, providence, or government
level. In an ideal court-based situation, the decision-making parties
are unbiased and unaffected by the actions or influence of all who are
involved in the case or are being judged. By establishing this anonym-
ity of a procedure, the actions of both the defendant and prosecutor
are weighed by their morals, and an accurate decision regarding their
consequences is made by the judge. As God has it, He is able to do the
same on a spiritual level. Therefore, with the knowledge of previous
corruption and defiance created on earth by the watchers' interference,
God shall determine their final resting place appropriately.

With these parables, the lessons in loyalty to the Lord or the decision
to stay on the right path in life are laid out clearly for those who wish
to avoid the same fate as the Watchers. Enoch's parables explain that
when the Lord himself deems it fit to do so, there will be a time for all
souls to be judged and placed to rest. From highly revered leaders and
kings to the most humble of people. In this sense, the lessons learned
from the parables can be considered in nearly all situations and not
just the ones that were laid before Enoch in his time. In this particular story, the actions taken by the watchers had corrupted humans

through the creation of the Nephilim, causing a chain of events that would require a cleansing of the world to find balance again. Similarly, in modern times the instances of similar actions being taken may be debatable when it comes to human lives, but there are also instances of a similar pattern emerging from nature at times in this desire to recreate balance in an environment that lacks it. As Enoch's parables continue, the Son of Man, presumably Jesus, is envisioned with God as they reside in their heavenly dwelling.

Not only does this preview what visions Enoch will have of heaven that are yet to come in the Book of Enoch, but it reassures that the judgments of all souls will be done under pure intentions and righteousness. Finally, the third parable emerges as a promise to those who are true. In response to their loyalty, the Lord states that their spirits would have the rights of peace, living in blessing and free from darkness.

CHAPTER THREE:

BOOK OF THE LUMINARIES

[Enoch 72 – 82]

Chapter Three:

Book of the Luminaries

In the book of the Luminaries, Enoch is shown the inner workings of distinguishing the days, seasons, and everything else recorded through the use of a 364-day calendar system by the Archangel Uriel. Beginning the book of the Luminaries, Enoch is granted the vision to detect many of the heavenly bodies we know today, such as the sun, moon, and all the stars in our solar system, in addition to their pathways and patterns they take while they travel through space. As these patterns are noticed, so is the detail and care in which they remain the same, following strict and divine laws that never falter. Naturally, Enoch is able to think further about this idea and respect the ebb and flow of the earth's seasons and continuity.

In the generalization of the ideas of Biblical creation and the concept of interstellar 'Big Bang' theories, many find the two opposing each other, where in reality, these beliefs could very well be complimentary. The study of scientific subjects in nearly any topic are working theories or educational assumptions pieced together like a puzzle to bring an answer to an unsolved question or phenomena. In biology, for example, animals are classified due to their physical and internal characteristics and similarities, but that does not mean that their categories of genus or even species are finite. We have mammals that are broadly defined as having hair and mammary glands, with most giving birth to live offspring, but there are exceptions who lay eggs instead (such as the platypus). We classify snakes as reptiles that lack legs, but ancient snakes have been found to have their own appendages once. To summarize, science is constantly changing as we learn of the natural occurrences in our world and work to understand their heavenly design.

Regarding the 'Big Bang Theory,' in short, the foundation this theory lies upon is the idea of sudden creation out of vast emptiness. In simple terms, God's depiction of creation and the big bang relies on the synopsis of a huge amount of energy being released, forming what we know today as our galaxy. Would it be that much more of a stretch to consider the narrative of God creating the universe at this time, as He also began the Old Testament with the perception of expansion through emptiness? The comparison of the two is worth a review in the least, regardless of which side of the argument one is on. One final supporting factor in this comparison is the measurement of time in regards to when all of this occurred. For both events, we do not actually have a set period of time from the beginning of the start of the universe, and so estimations and perspectives come into play. God's creation of the universe supposedly happened on the first day, but the term 'day' in itself can relationally be understood not as an exact measurement of a 24-hour period but a loose term of measurement for us to understand what the Lord meant to tell us. Similarly, there is not much that can be proven yet on how long it took for the big bang to come to fruition, leaving time up to the interpretation of each person. Regardless, as our technology advances, it will be interesting to uncover new information about our physical and spiritual origins.

Continuing on the subject of time, historically, there are many instances of cultures keeping track of time in many ways, from sundials to the changing of the season and even efforts to chart and map celestial bodies in rough (yet oftentimes accurate) interpretations. In the days of Jesus Christ, there was no true mention of time in terms of seconds, hours, or minutes, as many people in that era did not yet have such a rigid form of calculating their times of the day. Additionally, it is also notable that devices such as sundials were not common for the average person of the time, as only more wealthy leaders or kings would have them in their possession. Instead of modern timekeeping, the term hour was used as a definition for a multitude of stretches of time, even including whole spans of days or seasons!

For practical purposes in these times of Jesus and Enoch's time before him, celestial bodies such as the sun and moon were important in their keeping of time and direction in practical means, such as scheduling a time to meet with others or beginnings of certain events. Although we are very much used to the rigidities of time that our modern society uses now, some situations still require this biblical method of tracking time. Imagine backpacking in a secluded wilderness area, such as a forest. In many cases, these areas do not have modern cell signals to keep track of time, so if one had ventured off without a second time-keeping device, such as a watch, the only method to estimate how much time had passed would be by these similar methods. As long as one had visibility to the sky above them, they would be able to distinguish the difference between night and day, therefore telling the rough estimate of the time that had passed based on the location of the celestial bodies in the sky. In a well-versed outdoors person, even accurate directions could be determined based on the constants of patterns that the stars, sun, and moon all follow. As for other methods of keeping time, the seasons would be of much significance and accuracy. Not only did they set the guidelines for methods in calculating other methods of keeping time later on, but seasonal differences could be measured overall by changes in temperature, migration patterns, and other changes that all people could view on earth that God had arranged. Today, although we have precise measurements of time to keep track of our daily activities, our biological processes still have their ways of measuring time through circadian rhythm or your internal clock. With the general exception of our own circadian rhythms and routine, our own timekeeping is not without fault, as nearly every ancient calendar would often have small differential mistakes. Today, these errors are fixed as best as possible, but as one may notice, there are still hiccups regarding dates (i.e., the concept of leap years) and even regional time keeping (from time zones and the existence or lack of daylight savings).

Ever since the start of humanity, God has given all of us an important tool in order for us to understand when the time is right for vital processes such as eating and sleeping. Simply put, this mechanism, widely known as an internal clock, is responsible for the physical and mental changes that one goes through within a 24-hour period. This process marks when it's time to wake up and be active, all the way to the induction of sleepiness as the day gets later and turns to night. Of course, our modern lives and environment may affect these processes, but for the most part, if all distractions were removed, these patterns would be more apparent.

Similar to our own experience, many vertebrate animals are also reliant on an internal clock. One common example is found right on the average farm in poultry. As chickens are free to roam during the day, farmers are typically blessed with the utilization of these birds' internal clocks, since as the days wear down, most chickens will take themselves back to their barn in order to roost for the night, keeping them safe from predators and right on schedule, and making our own internal clocks a key part in determining a measurement for time.

In Enoch's time, not all people were well-versed in the ideas and mathematics involved in navigation or determining any aspect of time down to the second, making the first vision given to Enoch that much more unique and extraordinary. With this vision, Enoch is able to grasp the concepts of a calendar system of years, as well as the tracking of the days, months, years, and seasons. Understandably so, Enoch was in awe of the meticulous details that the Lord had created, so as the patterns and ellipses of each and every nearby star revealed themselves as being constant and planned in great detail, it isn't much of a surprise that Enoch had been accompanied by the Archangel Uriel who could offer help and understanding.

This point in Enoch's series of visions is notably the first time for the introduction of Uriel and their interactions with Enoch. From an assortment of biblical texts and even the Book of Enoch itself, we know that Uriel is deemed the Archangel of wisdom and a master of all knowledge (and presumably its' safekeeping as well, since Uriel is also noted to be one of the Archangels guarding over Tartarus, chasm-like imprisonment meant for fallen angels such as the Watchers). Featured in future scripts of both Christian and Jewish texts alike, Uriel is often depicted with a book or scroll in hand, representing their responsibility for safeguarding and interpreting knowledge.

According to the beginning of the fall of the watchers, Uriel was also named as one of the archangels calling out to God in retaliation, advocating for the benefits of restoring the balance for mankind in a world becoming corrupt by sin. Of course, these pleas didn't go unanswered, as God then decided to begin His plan of action to cleanse the earth of the Watchers, their violence-prone offspring of Nephilim, and any other cruelty or suffering that had begun as a result of their interference in the world of humans. Later on, as Enoch begins to emerge into his blessings of receiving the knowledge of God's plans to cleanse the world through his visions, he is also guided in part by Uriel throughout his journey of understanding what was being described. Later on, according to some scripture accounts, Uriel is last seen interacting with Enoch's descendant, Noah, as the time is closer to prepare for the Great Flood, further ensuring that the word of God was not lost in translation between generations and would give Uriel the nickname of the Archangel of Prophecies.

"And now, my son, I have shown thee everything, and the law of all the stars of the heaven is [2] completed. And he showed me all the laws of these for every day, and for every season of bearing rule, and for every year, and for its going forth, and for the order prescribed to it every month [3] and every week: And the waning of the moon which takes place in the sixth portal: for in this [4] sixth portal her light is accomplished, and after that there is the beginning of the waning: (And the waning) which takes place in the first portal in its season, till one hundred and seventy-seven [5] days are accomplished: reckoned according to weeks, twenty-five (weeks) and two days. She falls behind the sun and the order of the stars exactly five days in the course of one period, and when [6] this place which thou seest has been traversed. Such is the picture and sketch of every luminary which Uriel the archangel, who is their leader, showed unto me."

By this time, Enoch had come to the conclusion of the patterns and repetitions that make up the workings of all celestial bodies, just as astrologers of ancient and modern times work to understand the same concepts. As Enoch understands his new studies in the patterns of the luminaries, Uriel the Archangel points out a significant comparison between the obedience of the luminaries and the disobedience of man. The patterns that aligned perfectly with the laws of nature provided by the Lord had caused the Luminaries to continuously follow them without faltering, regardless of the situation. With this, Uriel then explains that humankind has a similar gradient of patterns and rules set by God to keep them on the path towards blessings as well. Similar to the Luminaries, if one remained as regular and unfaltering as possible under the guise of the will of God, they would be blessed. On the other hand, if one were to envelop themselves in sin and disobedience, they would not be able to count on any rewards or good fortune. Uriel's explanation of the rulings of behavior that are tied to worthiness in the eyes of the Lord allowed Enoch to grasp further the situation and direness of consequences faced by those who do not listen to these rulings, now explained as clear as day.

For example, as a young child, the capacity and understanding of concepts may be limited at first. A toddler may not fully understand why a cooking pan is hot yet are told it is dangerous and not good to touch. With enough of a simple explanation, the toddler has a higher chance of understanding this danger and would be more likely to follow their parents' orders, but if an explanation is not clear for any reason, the toddler's curious and impulsive nature might get the better of them leading to a sharp, fast lesson of their consequences.

Similarly, if the toddler understood the information clearly and still decided to reach out in defiance, the same consequences are met. In this case and in a metaphorical sense, the laws and physics of a hot pan would act as God's judgment towards sinful actions. To assist their understanding and potentially keep them from these dangers, Uriel, or the parent, attempts to step in and define what the entire situation means, and eventually, by the free choice of the child, the resulting effects would be determined.

"And in the days of the sinners the years shall be shortened,
And their seed shall be tardy on their lands and fields,
And all things on the earth shall alter,
And shall not appear in their time:
And the rain shall be kept back
And the heaven shall withhold (it).
3 And in those times the fruits of the earth shall be backward,
And shall not grow in their time,
And the fruits of the trees shall be withheld in their time.
4 And the moon shall alter her order,
And not appear at her time.
And in those days the sun shall be seen and he shall journey in the evening
*   on the extremity of the great chariot in the west*
And shall shine more brightly than accords with the order of light.
6 And many chiefs of the stars shall transgress the order (prescribed).
And these shall alter their orbits and tasks,
And not appear at the seasons prescribed to them.
7 And the whole order of the stars shall be concealed from the sinners,
And the thoughts of those on the earth shall err concerning them,
[And they shall be altered from all their ways],
Yea, they shall err and take them to be gods.
8 And evil shall be multiplied upon them,
And punishment shall come upon them So as to destroy all."

After these extraordinary experiences, Enoch then records what he has experienced in a series of books to Methuselah, who will further preserve them for keeping and sharing the knowledge the Lord gave Enoch through those past experiences and visions. Although not quite yet in the story themselves, it is best to note that Methuselah is a descendant of Enoch, more specifically his future son, who would be burdened with a smaller but still important part of carrying out God's desires of cleansing the world of the Nephilim and watchers. In time, Methuselah would fulfill his duties in family and fatherhood, eventually fathering Lamech, another minor yet key part of the continuation of their family line. Finally, it is important to note that with this duty of the family, Methuselah was blessed with an extraordinarily long-life span. Rivaling that of all who lived before and after him, Methuselah had only passed once he reached the mature age of 969 years.

While Methuselah plays a larger part later in the comings of Noah (notably, Noah is his grandson) through the books of Genesis and later through mentions in the Gospel of Luke, Enoch himself would rely on Methuselah to carry his stories, as Enoch will eventually pass at the age of 365. With the luminaries set as one of the shortest chapters regarding the Book of Enoch, it brings a strong transition to the telling of Enoch's visions he had previously experienced through his dreams.

"I have given Wisdom to thee and to thy children,
[And thy children that shall be to thee],
That they may give it to their children for generations,
This wisdom (namely) that passeth their thought.
³ And those who understand it shall not sleep,
But shall listen with the ear that they may learn this wisdom,
And it shall please those that eat thereof better than good food."

Altogether, Enoch's experience and vision of the inner workings of the heavenly luminaries brought the ideas he already understood about God's initial creation of the universe to light (pun intended). He then began to understand the significance of the complexity of these patterns and cycles, especially as the Lord had arranged everything just as it should be. Making Earth not only able to carry life but to support and let it flourish in the long run.

Finally, regarding Enoch's visions and comprehension of the luminaries in this chapter, the thought-provoking question as to the origination of the universe is brought up as well under modern, scientific understandings. What became of this was the uncanny resemblance between one of the most well-known theories of universe creation, the big bang, being compared to the first day of God's creation. As previously mentioned, both hold strong arguments that, on the surface, may seem conflicting in the minds of scholars and theologists, but as they both offer the idea of a sudden influx of energy creating a reaction and eventual development of celestial bodies, the resemblance is worth pondering.

CHAPTER FOUR:

THE DREAM VISIONS

[Enoch 83 – 90]

Chapter Four:

The Dream Visions

At this point through Enoch's journey, he has gained insight into the established guarantees heaven has to offer, the consequences and darkness that is set aside for angels and humans who have caused great harm with no intention of redemption, and all the patterns of the universe through the ongoing, steady change of the seasons caused by the luminaries such as the sun, moon, and stars. In addition to these understandings brought to Enoch by God and his Archangels, Enoch had also been blessed with visions of how the world will change through a mass event of judgment due to the Watchers disobeying the Lord and descending from the heavens to partake in creating their own volatile offspring with humans. According to his vision, Enoch's descendant, Noah, would become the catalyst to create a vessel to spare all that is still true in the world as a great event would cleanse the Earth of its corruption.

Although Enoch's journey may seem daunting in the extensive longevity and details it includes, an easy way to think of his journey is through story-driven methods, such as television or video games. In the first episode, or level, the basics of what you may need to know to understand the context of the story, such as characters and settings. The Book of Enoch doesn't directly mention their settings and character right off the beginning, but from what we know through the Old Testament and other documents such as the Dead Sea Scrolls, scientists and historians are able to estimate the average range of time that the days of Enoch had been set in. Going from Enoch's historical lineage in ancestry, we are also able to estimate approximately how far back these days have gone through generations. Despite the establishment of years that had passed relative to these characters' ages, this concept is still debatable in terms of how it would translate into our modern methods of timekeeping but provides an outline of our tracking regardless (as seen in the previous chapter, these ages will still be depicted as years or however the source text has worded them for simplicity's sake). As Enoch moves toward what he is envisioning due to his blessing from God, the story progresses into another chapter, adding more complexity and depth to what Enoch had experienced.

In Enoch [83 to 90], Enoch is beginning to recollect all that he had experienced within his dreamlike visions to his son Methuselah in order for them to act as a segue or connection between the visions of the past and the actions that must be taken in the future. To begin, Enoch recollects his first vision of a great flood, bringing destruction upon all that was wicked on the earth and making it whole again. It's important to note that although Enoch had understood the events of this seeming disaster of an event, he did not yet know of the methods by which Noah would eventually evade this danger, as God later guided Noah to finding the answer and then blessing Noah's venture later on.

Noah, one of the most iconic figures in the Bible for both Christians and non-Christians alike, is the star of arguably one of the most notorious stories in the world. From murals of his deeds painted on nursery rooms to more in-depth analyses such as this book and others like it, Noah's story of building the ark has inspired hundreds of thousands across the world and can be reiterated anywhere from Sunday schools and lectures to tourist attractions and Hollywood cinemas. According to both the Bible and Book of Enoch, Noah would soon be the final descendant with a direct line to Adam. More specifically, being the tenth generation before the events of the Great Flood had occurred. In terms of more recent genealogy, Noah is related to Enoch through their patriarchal line, as Noah's father, Lamech, was born from Methuselah, who was the son of Enoch himself (and notably had lived the longest, as mentioned in former chapters).

As many already have learned, Noah's role in God's plan was to follow his guidance and direction (once through the transcriptions preserving Enoch's words to Methuselah and later in the form of his own visions with the Lord) in creating one final method of salvation from the oncoming flood. With this, God's intentions in creating the Great Flood was not with ill-intentions but with a desire and need to bring change into a corrupt world ravaged by the Watchers and their illegitimate offspring, as well as the evils and destruction that humans who turned to wrongdoing were involved in. Of course, with this need for a great cleansing of the world in order to preserve the pure creation that was a human being, there must be a method of keeping future generations of humans and animals safe from any harm. Under this requirement, God sent out a message to Enoch regarding the blessings his great-grandchild would pursue.

As the time passes on earth, He also reaches back toward Noah, as the Book of Enoch states that through Uriel, an archangel of the Lord, Noah is able to begin to learn of his duties and responsibility in creating a haven for those who must be cared for during the flood. As a result, Noah then begins to construct his iconic ark, a boat meant to withhold dozens of species of animals in addition to Noah's own family. Reasonably so, Noah's ark was built to the specifications he had been given by the Lord, making it sound and sturdy with the ability to withhold days of nonstop rough waters. After Noah's long and arduous journey upon the ark came to a conclusion, he then resumed his regular offerings to God and was told to continue to regrow the population of the earth again.

Although Noah was righteous and noble in his own acts, the inclusion of Enoch's visions and documentation in the Book of Enoch played a vital part in ensuring that Noah would have the proper foundational upbringing to get him to this point of achievement. As it will be explained later on in the dissection of the Book of Enoch, Noah wasn't always revered as a hero, and just the opposite was coming to mind as he was born of this world. According to the depictions mentioned of a newborn Noah through Enoch and his son Methuselah's eyes, the second Noah was born, he seemed as though he was not entirely average. As such, Noah's pale, whitened complexion, in comparison to his relatives' warmer tones combined with his unique aura, caused his father Lamech and grandfather Methuselah to worry their child was actually birthed in part from the Watchers themselves. Fortunately for all parties involved, they decided to seek out the wisdom of Enoch, who then was able to explain that through a righteous vision, he understood what this had meant and further assured them that Noah's appearance was not something to be worrisome, but was actually a signifier that he would become a righteous man himself, sent to assist the Lord in his need for a preservation method and reintroduction of species into the world after the flood.

"Two visions I saw before I took a wife, and the one was quite unlike the other: the first when I was learning to write: the second before I took thy mother, (when) I saw a terrible 3 vision. And regarding them I prayed to the Lord. I had laid me down in the house of my grandfather Mahalalel, (when) I saw in a vision how the heaven collapsed and was borne off and fell to 4 the earth. And when it fell to the earth, I saw how the earth was swallowed up in a great abyss, and mountains were suspended on mountains, and hills sank down on hills, and high trees were rent 5 from their stems, and hurled down and sunk in the abyss. And thereupon a word fell into my mouth, 6 and I lifted up (my voice) to cry aloud, and said: 'The earth is destroyed.' And my grandfather Mahalalel waked me as I lay near him, and said unto me: 'Why dost thou cry so, my son, and why 7 dost thou make such lamentation?' And I recounted to him the whole vision which I had seen, and he said unto me: 'A terrible thing hast thou seen, my son, and of grave moment is thy dream-vision as to the secrets of all the sin of the earth: it must sink into the abyss and be destroyed with 8 a great destruction. And now, my son, arise and make a petition to the Lord of glory, since thou art a believer, that a remnant may remain on the earth, and that He may not destroy the whole 9 earth."

As Enoch recollects, he mentions this first vision, as understandable and frightful as the destruction may be, but had been able to find more understanding and solace in prayer for guidance. Enoch's second vision is that of the watchers and their corruption. This is told in the metaphor of the emergence of a single bull and heifer from the ground. As the cattle begin to proliferate across the earth, a star is seen falling, leading to the first instance of betrayal from the angels to God. This first star is seen to darken a single bull, most likely Cain, to begin its spread of suffering, and not a long time afterward, more stars follow their lead and begin to impregnate other heifers of the world, causing the creation of violent, bloodthirsty creatures that then decided to lay waste to the earth, causing more pain and destruction.

Another modern example of what God is portraying to Enoch, the corruption of good into evil and wrongdoing, can be seen as a contagious illness like the common cold or a slowly growing mold. In these cases, all it takes to disrupt the natural balance of life is a single microorganism to attach itself to a suitable person or environment. From there, if it is not taken care of in a prompt manner, it has the chance to spread. That tiny germ picked up in one individual's hand may spread to other objects in their grasp, into their own body, and even spread to a friend with a simple gesture of touch. Likewise, a minuscule spore of mold finding itself in just the right conditions can proliferate into a colony, growing quickly and vastly until the time comes for it to be eradicated.

In the concept of sin being transferred from Cain, the original holder of corruption by man, to the heifer, the concept is very similar and can be seen even in today's society. Us humans are very social, and we often take cues from the actions of those around us in the proper way to act. In most cases, we are told through our caretakers at a very young age what is right and wrong, therefore adding to our own inner compass of morality. The emergence of sin and wrongdoing, however, warps the vision of what is the right thing to do. Under this influence, people begin only to consider their own well-being or immediate desires, leaving goals and welfare behind. In turn, the temptation of others witnessing these actions and what their immediate 'reward' had resulted in, they are more likely to attempt it on their own, similar to peer pressure.

Imagine going to the grocery store with a friend and waiting in the checkout line. Many times, shops offer small candies and trinkets and commonly grab last-minute purchases near the aisles, but this time you notice your friend snag a candy bar from the shelf and swiftly stash it in their pocket. Most of us are not innately inclined to steal for no reason, so the thought of a friend doing so and bearing witness to the crime would be shocking and conflicting. Do you let it pass as though it didn't happen, or do you confront the friend? The decision is even more difficult as the friend may reassure you that there is no way for them to get caught and encourages you to grab your favorite candy too. On the surface, this newfound sin of unnecessary theft is shocking, but human curiosity and the desire to remain in good relationships with someone you care about can easily shift one's morals towards wanting to be included by participating.

As time goes by, this sin has the potential to grow and spread, just as Cain's first seeds of corruption had, albeit the latter was presumably more destructive and harmful than the former. Regardless, if one gains immediate satisfaction with their wrongly chosen actions, in this case, earning a free candy bar, it can quickly become a slippery slope towards sharing this behavior with others or even repeating the same actions over and over.

Although this recollection is a metaphorical vision of what was occurring through the creation of giants, or Nephilim, that caused such great destruction and chaos, it is also known as the Animal Apocalypse as the cattle representing a man on earth in Enoch's vision were depicted struggling with their own experiences of corruption. After this second vision comes Enoch's third and final vision to share with his son Methuselah; the complete vision of what is next to come for those who were caught in the crossfire or remained true to the Lord in what would seem like a forsaken world.

Enoch's final vision opens with the image of two temples, one that is new and bright and another that appears discarded, unkempt and unclean. In this vision, there were not only cattle but animals of all kinds that began to journey to the newly formed temple, all the while proliferating to create more of themselves, including a notable group of twelve sheep. Throughout their journey, these sheep remained faithful and willing to call upon the Lord when they encountered danger, and the Lord responded by providing them with the protection they needed, whether it be from wolves, boar, or any other dangers.

"And I saw that a white bull was born, with large horns and all the beasts of the field and all the [38] birds of the air feared him and made a petition to him all the time. And I saw till all their generations were transformed, and they all became white bulls; and the first among them became a lamb, and that lamb became a great animal and had great black horns on its head; and the Lord of the sheep [39] rejoiced over it and over all the oxen. And I slept in their midst: and I awoke and saw everything. [40] This is the vision which I saw while I slept, and I awoke and blessed the Lord of righteousness and [41] gave Him glory. Then I wept with a great weeping and my tears stayed not till I could no longer endure it: when I saw, they flowed on account of what I had seen; for everything shall come and [42] be fulfilled, and all the deeds of men in their order were shown to me. On that night I remembered the first dream, and because of it, I wept and was troubled–because I had seen that vision."

Finally, as these animals all reached the shining new temple, it was clear that although they may not all be perfect in an ideal way, they did not falter in their loyalty and persistence in attempting to better themselves and their world. Once reaching this new house, it appeared that the animals, big and small, had the opportunity to transform themselves through the power of a powerful white bull, who had re-cast each animal in the image of the Lord, alluding to the eventual coming of the Son of God and the salvation of all.

On a looser comparison, this vision of the collection of numerous types of animals proceeding through the two temples (representing two choices in good and glory, or evil and sin) and all of their following conflicts among each other can also be compared to the entirety of the history of humanity. Beginning with the creation of the bovine representations of the figures Adam and Eve, the beginning of animal-kind and humanity respectfully, it is fair to see the ebb and flow of events such as the fall of the Watchers, the birth of Nephilim, and even the three major turning points in judgment as to the story of the animal apocalypse rolls towards their conclusion. In this case, after the events of Noah's flooding, there would come a time of redemption for all again, and afterward, as a final wave of wicked doings encroached upon humans once more, a final savior would eventually be realized as the Son of God and last chance for redemption.

In the case of the candy bar theft example, it is vital to know that those who had attempted to follow in the footsteps of theft that the friend had (and those who came before the friend) would also be treated as the cattle in Enoch's vision had; with repentance and forgiveness. As God has explained many times over in both the Book of Enoch and numerous other encounters, texts, and documents, He is of a forgiving nature. As long as one desires to realize and repent their wrongdoings and strive to better themselves by avoiding repeating their former action with authenticity, He will take that matter into perspective when the time comes to judge the entirety of a soul.

CHAPTER FIVE:

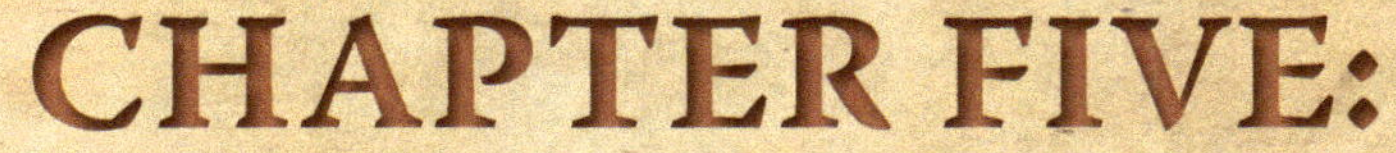

THE EPISTLE OF ENOCH

[Enoch 91 -105]

CHAPTER FIVE:

THE EPISTLE OF ENOCH

Finally, after describing all of his prior visions, Enoch set forth to create a final message to his son Methuselah and his family. At this point, Enoch is visited with his final vision of his own final resting place through ascension into heaven. By finalizing his story with this last vision, Enoch offers some guidance to his family and all that desire to remain true and achieve the same blessings from life to death.

To clarify the endpoint of Enoch's final journey, in the Book of Enoch, it is not actually explicitly stated that Enoch had physically passed away in common sense, as there are many references that state Enoch, even at his old age, did not experience death. According to the Book of Enoch and other biblical references discovered at various points in our modern history, the concept of bypassing the physical aspects of death is very rare, but not unheard of, as two other key figures have experienced this phenomenon; Elijah and Jesus himself. In the case of Elijah, his ascension to heaven was one of the more sudden and debatable events, as a depiction of a flaming chariot had appeared and beckoned him to ascend. Compared to Enoch's ascension before the events of Elijah's time had taken place, the recollection of Elijah's scenario is still in debate regarding the specifics of what occurred due to this sudden nature as well. Many also debate the language used in the description of the ascension of Elijah, as some interpretations define it as a disappearance *similar* to ascension into heaven instead of a literal account of the ascension. All that being said, unless more information and documentation can be found in the future, we may never know if Elijah had ascended just as Enoch did centuries before.

One final and finite example of ascending to heaven from Earth can be found in the story of Jesus Christ himself. In Christ's case, his ascension only began as he had completed all of his duties on Earth among humans. After the events of his graceful means of assisting those in need all the way to the conclusion of his crucifixion and resurrection, Jesus had walked and lived as any man had in his day. Later, as he had fulfilled all these duties of forgiveness and repentance from his selfless sacrifice, Jesus eventually understood that his time on Earth was coming to a close. In order to continue God's work of righteousness, approximately forty days after his resurrection, Jesus then continued his goals in judgment and overall management in the heavens by finally ascending and returning to his Father. Afterwards, many who had encountered his presence or good deeds upon earth rushed to give their praise and thanks to God, as His son was their salvation in a harsh world.

To further support the evidence of Enoch and Elijah's ascension, however, many researchers believe that the scripture of Revelations holds the chronological connection between Christ and the two righteous men. In this section, an audience of two witnesses who soon emerge to reveal themselves account of the deeds and goodwill of Jesus shortly before he arrives on Earth for the second time. Although there is not much to determine the identities of these two witnesses, one plausible option is that they are Enoch and Elijah, as they are the only other biblical figures who had been given the privilege of ascending to heaven as Christ would do after them. No matter the future who experienced it, the true meaning of ascension alludes to the accuracy of the Lord's timing in the completion of events or duties on earth by a righteous figure and finally offering them spiritual rest.

"*² Let not your spirit be troubled on account of the times;
For the Holy and Great One has appointed days for all things.*

[3] And the righteous one shall arise from sleep,
[Shall arise] and walk in the paths of righteousness,
And all his path and conversation shall be in eternal goodness and grace.
[4] He will be gracious to the righteous and give him eternal uprightness,
And He will give him power so that he shall be (endowed) with goodness
  and righteousness.
And he shall walk in eternal light.
[5] And sin shall perish in darkness for ever,
And shall no more be seen from that day for evermore."

As Enoch's experience has shown through visions of the fall of the Watchers all the way through the coming and emergence of salvation for the innocent, through the destruction and chaos that darkness had brought upon the world still comes a time for rebalancing it as well. Just as how a storm may leave wreckage behind in its path, obscuring what areas were once covered in beauty, or how a wildfire can rip through forests in an instant, the passage of time and the efforts of doing good will reinvent and restore the area's natural wonders. Debris can be cleared, ashes can blow away in the wind, and new life can emerge stronger and brighter than ever.

In the Book of Enoch, the metaphorical storm that Enoch's family and even the whole world were attempting to outlast was the downfall and destruction left by the Watchers' actions. Just as high winds tear and fray all that become trapped in it, the Watchers' descent into creating their own human-esque lives on Earth had begun to wear good-willed humans down to their final limits of hope and faith in the Lord. Likewise, those who were tempted by the corruption that the Watchers and their Nephilim offspring had caused had decided to join in their own chaos-causing plans, primarily for their own benefit.

In order to brave this storm, Enoch was then gifted one of the most important tools that could be used to thwart these pressures of darkness; the gift of knowledge. Afterward, it was clear to Enoch that this figurative and occasionally literal storm would have to be endured for quite a significant amount of time as the Lord had everything prepared and planned out. Regardless, Enoch's determination to be a righteous man led him to be stoic in his faith, patiently understanding that although he may not truly see the end himself before the time came for him to ascend to heaven, his children would need his exact words and guidance to reassure their responsibilities and role to play. Eventually, all of this faith and patience pay off, just as Enoch was told, as his great-grandson Noah is eventually born towards the end of Enoch's time, with a great distinction in his physical and spiritual presence marking him for greatness.

Further on in the time after both Enoch and Noah's experience, Enoch also becomes aware through his visions of a final chance for forgiveness in the perspective of a spirit's judgment day. Although Noah and the rest of Enoch's descendants had worked hard and faithfully in fulfilling their duties in order for the Great Flood to be surpassed by humankind, there would still be more challenges yet to come, as kings and leaders are tempted with sinful desires of greed in wealth and power. Naturally, the common folk weren't isolated from these trends in corrupted behavior, as even the average person could become twisted into dark, selfish behavior as well. As a result of this plague that had continued to grow, even after the Great Flood resolved the issue of fallen angels dwelling on earth, the Lord had decided to plan to send his Son, or a Son of Man, to bring light to the ways of sinners, eventually offering forgiveness and repentance for those who wanted to change themselves and seek a better way of living, both physically and spiritually.

Enoch's visions of the incidents that were yet to occur, the great change the Lord would need to cause through a flood to cleanse every corrupt corner of Enoch's world, and later the introduction of the messiah himself bringing salvation and forgiveness to even stronger sinful temptations humans had faced post-flood, is the utmost example of the exact preciseness the Lord works in, which was shown as virtually perfect in its timing. With all of the information he had obtained through his visions, Enoch now knows the importance of taking responsibility for one's own actions, as well as having faith in the plans of the Lord, regardless of if it is a measurable force for your own lifetime. Naturally, as Enoch explains all of these situations and experiences with his family, he emphasizes the need to remain steadfast and true, as well as keep this faith in their own respective righteous paths. Considering the record-keeping and knowledge of God is all-knowing in the affairs of everything on the earth, whenever one chose to commit any heinous sins or crimes against their fellow man, it was also important for Enoch to note that naturally these would also be recorded, since by the time that one faces their own session of judgment for their actions, all of their life would be considered as a whole to paint the picture of their true soul.

"Woe to you who work godlessness,
And glory in lying and extol them:
Ye shall perish, and no happy life shall be yours.
² Woe to them who pervert the words of uprightness,
And transgress the eternal law,
And transform themselves into what they were not [into sinners]:
They shall be trodden under foot upon the earth.
³ In those days make ready, ye righteous, to raise your prayers as a memorial,
And place them as a testimony before the angels,
That they may place the sin of the sinners for a memorial before the
  Most High.
⁴ In those days the nations shall be stirred up,
And the families of the nations shall arise on the day of destruction.
⁵ And in those days the destitute shall go forth and carry off their children,
And they shall abandon them, so that their children shall perish through
  them:
Yea, they shall abandon their children (that are still) sucklings, and not
  return to them,
And shall have no pity on their beloved ones."

As further guided similarly to the rules of the ten commandments, Enoch mentions that idealization and materialism are to be avoided as well, as the general rule of respect for the Lord and all that He created would be to avoid falsehoods that may lead one astray or cloud true guidance and vision. Overall, Enoch stresses the importance of practicing righteousness in society and one's own morals as the wickedness and cruelty that attempts to envelop the world are judged in both an upcoming flood of change through Noah's story and in another mass era of judgment yet to come.

Just as our modern understandings of the Bible state, true materialism is depicted as a mix of sins that bring about greed, pride, and many other toxic traits that can not only distract one from positive intentions and impact but can become an uncontrollable storm of destruction in its more extreme cases. To explain more clearly, it is not a sinful act to have possessions in themselves (although some challenge themselves on even this and strive towards minimizing their possessions to the bare minimum), as many of us do have objects around our homes in the hundreds to thousands in the count, but these situations can become sinful when the attachment and desire for objects surpass other personal values, such as friendship, family, and personal honor. In short, it is where we place our priorities in life that determine our character and, therefore, our own righteousness. Of course, nobody is perfect, the Lord knows that, but as Enoch began to understand through his visions, the true intentions of a soul are what determines their final statement in where they will rest.

"I know a mystery
And have read the heavenly tablets,
And have seen the holy books,
And have found written therein and inscribed regarding them:
³ That all goodness and joy and glory are prepared for them,
And written down for the spirits of those who have died in righteousness,
And that manifold good shall be given to you in recompense for your labours,
And that your lot is abundantly beyond the lot of the living.
⁴ And the spirits of you who have died in righteousness shall live and rejoice,
And their spirits shall not perish, nor their memorial from before the face
*   of the Great One*
Unto all the generations of the world: wherefore no longer fear their
*   contumely.*
5 Woe to you, ye sinners, when ye have died,
If ye die in the wealth of your sins,
And those who are like you say regarding you:
'Blessed are the sinners: they have seen all their days.

⁶ And how they have died in prosperity and in wealth,
And have not seen tribulation or murder in their life;
And they have died in honour,
And judgement has not been executed on them during their life."
⁷ Know ye, that their souls will be made to descend into Sheol
And they shall be wretched in their great tribulation.
⁸ And into darkness and chains and a burning flame where there is
*   grievous judgement shall your spirits enter;*
And the great judgement shall be for all the generations of the world.
Woe to you, for ye shall have no peace.
9 Say not in regard to the righteous and good who are in life:
" In our troubled days we have toiled laboriously and experienced every
*   trouble,*
And met with much evil and been consumed,
And have become few and our spirit small.
¹⁰ And we have been destroyed and have not found any to help us even
*   with a word:*
We have been tortured [and destroyed], and not hoped to see life from day
*   to day.*
¹¹ We hoped to be the head and have become the tail:
We have toiled laboriously and had no satisfaction in our toil;
And we have become the food of the sinners and the unrighteous,
And they have laid their yoke heavily upon us.
¹² They have had dominion over us that hated us and smote us;
And to those that hated us we have bowed our necks
But they pitied us not.
¹³ We desired to get away from them that we might escape and be at rest,
But found no place whereunto we should flee and be safe from them.
¹⁴ And are complained to the rulers in our tribulation,
And cried out against those who devoured us,
But they did not attend to our cries
And would not hearken to our voice."

With this last quote, Enoch concludes that after all judgment comes that final resting place for all spirits, good and bad. If one is determined to be a sincerely good soul, there will be a modest reward in that title. Not to be confused with riches and fame (which would be an extension of materialism in short), the type of rest and rewards that well-intended souls would experience is that of a lack of worry or need, as a place of safety and rest from a challenging life on earth. Imagining life on earth without struggle may seem as though it could be a physically impossible feat, but one must keep in mind that although it feels impossible, the Lord is strong in His word, especially as it comes to the judgment of spirits to their rightful place.

Conversely, as previously depicted, the results of living in sin unashamedly and for your own personal benefit will result in quite the opposite of a spiritual resting place. In this case, one would be faced with severe and apropos punishment for all of the wicked deeds that they had actively participated in and initiated.

The world in itself is full of challenges, survival, and even struggles at times, but just as Enoch had reassured his own family, one must have patience, understanding, and lastly, faith in not only your own outcome in life but faith in the goodness of life itself over temptation and corruption. In conclusion, if there are any morals and understandings not of historical chronology that can be taken away from the Book of Enoch, it's that God does have a plan and solution for everyone's benefit in the constant struggle for a balance between good and evil, no matter of if the timeline of doing so lines up perfectly with our manufactured concept of tracking time and events. In doing so, just as Enoch's family did, there is a sense of endurance one must take on this journey, as life will never be a sprint but a steady marathon to the finish line.

Finally, moving back to the analogy of a vengeful storm, one must understand that the opportunity for sin will nearly always be present, whether it's in the sense of temptation, desire, or even self-proclaimed 'shortcuts' one could take through life to reach an end goal. In most cases, this temptation won't bring much fulfillment in one's true desires or goals and will only impede that journey through life's struggles.

CHAPTER SIX:

THE BIRTH OF NOAH

[Enoch 106 – 107]

CHAPTER SIX:

THE BIRTH OF NOAH

Many are already well-acquainted with the story and life tellings of Noah, even if they do not necessarily identify as Christian, as the legend itself is an extraordinary feat of faith, endurance, and rebirth, taken in the form of refreshing the world's living organisms from corruption. From murals to children's toys garnished with imagery of the ark, many are well accustomed to the general idea of Noah and his goal from God to carry animals of each species upon it for days during the great flood. Although this is the most common image most think of, it does not explain the entirety of Noah's story. As we learn from the Book of Enoch (and later in chapters of Genesis), Noah's role to play in the entirety of God's plans is essential to their success. As far as his character, Noah is depicted in both the Book of Enoch and Genesis scriptures as one of the most righteous men of his time.

Generally, this explains why Noah was chosen to not only carry out God's desires to start anew after washing away all the wickedness of the world but explains his designation in preserving his own family and lineage to carry on with repopulation after these events had occurred. Overall, Noah is unchallenged as a figure of good and loyalty in the Old Testament, just as his family before him had been, but that doesn't mean that Noah was without any fault. On the contrary, the only biblical figure deemed perfect in every way is Jesus Christ himself. Regarding Noah, he had his challenges and struggles in life just as the majority of us do today. In Genesis, this can be seen as Noah, who had an affinity for drink, even to the point of maintaining his own winery for a time before the flood. Unfortunately, Noah had the habit of drinking quite too much at times, and on a handful of occasions, he would accidentally become too intoxicated, embarrassing his own sons by passing out in his sleeping tent for the night. Regardless of his personal struggles, with the grace of God, Noah was able to achieve feats unseen by any of his peers. More impressively, Noah was deemed to be about 500 years old at the time of living in the ark and would later live over 300 years after the incident of the flood, making him not as old as Enoch but still ranked as one of the oldest figures in Biblical times. Lastly, Noah found himself with just the right combinations of skills to complete the Lord's desire to build an ark. He was a farmer and ship maker, two trades that would show to be essential in not only creating the ark but preserving the welfare of those who would board it.

In summary, Noah's prominence in the tellings of the Old Testament section of the Bible begins with his encounter and guidance from the Lord to aid in His goals of cleansing the Earth from wickedness. At the time, all of the corruption brought onto the earth had increasingly been built up by the fallen Watchers through their desire to please themselves and act as humans. These would include activities such as taking their own human wives and exploiting the privileges of creating offspring.

In turn, these offspring (or Nephilim, as they are occasionally referred to) had been described as giants when compared to the average human, with a near insatiable level of bloodlust and desire for violence. This is the general understanding of Nehlilim's behavior through the Book of Enoch, but it is important to note that, like many other biblical tellings, there are variances in the details and morals intended by the Nephilim. Some depictions show them as more chaotic beings that could pose a threat to both humans and higher powers, but regardless of their intentions, the unanimous decision on all arguments states that in order for the world to return to a state of calm after the disruptions, all Nephilim would need to be eliminated.

With this knowledge in hand, the Lord turned to Enoch by blessing him with visions of how this unimaginable feat of saving the earth and its inhabitants would be solved. As the Lord determined, there would soon be a great flood intended to wash away all of the suffering and turmoil that was caused by the Watchers, and in order to re-establish a new, rejuvenated population, Enoch's own descendant, Noah, would be tasked with ensuring those who would be needed after the destruction was wiped clean. As many may already know, this included all varieties and species of animals, from the smallest bird to the largest mammals, and the rest is history.

Although the Book of Enoch only foretells the events of the great flood, the second to last segment in the entire catalog refers to the depictions of the Birth of Noah, son of Lamech, grandson of Methuselah, and great-grandson of Enoch himself. When Noah had finally been born, he was noted as being a child with an odd appearance for the times. Noah's skin and hair were depicted as white as snow, with a rosy undertone and shining bright eyes that lit up the room and were compared to the rays of the sun. The information we have on Noah's appearance is still in the debate at times and may require more insight, but with this description and further context found from the Dead Sea Scrolls, many have considered the possibility that Noah may have been born with albinism, especially as his appearance was emphasized as not of the norm for his time.

Regardless of the circumstances, Noah's father, Lamech's initial reaction was somewhat in shock at his extraordinary child that was just born. He then decided to seek guidance from his own father and grandfather as to why Noah's appearance and demeanor seemed more fitting towards a heavenly being instead of a human. Methuselah and Lamech's anxieties were finally calmed as Enoch had described that instead of fear and worry, hope and rejoicing was to be the best course of action. With this, Enoch had begun to explain and clarify his vision of what was still yet to come per God's will. In order to rid the earth of all the corruption the fallen angels had previously caused through their disobedience, a great flooding was planned to emerge, but in order to preserve the goodness and the ones who were still loyal and true,

Noah would be the one to follow the Lord and find a way to withstand the temporary turmoil.

Enoch explained that with this great change, nearly an entire year would come to pass where Noah's solution would have to withstand these trials until relief would be found. Despite this, Noah would not be alone, as he would be blessed and guided by the Lord Himself, with his own children by his side. Finally, Enoch explained that with this era of change will come a time for balance in the world again. This wouldn't come as a paradise on earth, as this great flooding was classified as the first of two major reassessments in judgment for all living creatures. The intention of this initial cleansing was to rid the land of those who were born from disobedience by the Watchers and who have continued that legacy through violence and chaos. In conclusion, the final day of judgment for all human beings was still yet to come and not of Noah's time but much further on. With this newfound understanding of their father's premonition, Methuselah and Lamech rejoiced in the good their unique child Noah would eventually bring.

CHAPTER SEVEN:

The Final Book of Enoch

[Enoch 108]

CHAPTER SEVEN:

THE FINAL BOOK OF ENOCH

Chapter 108, the final passage documenting the guidance from the explanations of Enoch's revelations, summarize the lessons that must be actively learned and followed from the actions brought by the fallen angels along with their inevitable destruction and wickedness brought to Earth. This final book documented by Enoch was a direct message for his son Methuselah in order to bring him and his descendants' wisdom and a plan of action for the days to come. From his initial journey in envisioning the changes that will soon come to pass in the world, Enoch's opportunity to follow the will of God and share his experiences would not be disregarded.

In modern times, this guidance that Enoch had issues with his family could be loosely compared to a will of an elderly relative. Not including physical possessions or specific regional laws, many will often have a final message or set of guidelines that the deceased had wanted to pass down to their family, whether it's a message of encouragement, a loving goodbye, or a major reveal of their life as a whole. For Enoch, this means ensuring his own generational lineage has heard the word of God as he did through his visions and had the tools capable of carrying out his (and by extension, God's) will as time passed. At this point in time, Enoch himself had begun preparing to reach the end of his journey, ready to ascend to heaven and be with the Lord for the rest of his days. It's important to note that throughout the Book of Enoch, it is not clear if Enoch had passed away in a traditional sense or had gone through a more literal ascension into heaven just from the text, but regardless he would find himself in a situation where physical reach towards his family and future generations was not possible, meaning passing on his message for the preparation of the Lord's plans was of the utmost importance. Although there is some uncertainty in the details of the departure of Enoch into the heavens, his final documents and message were well-received.

Our time on the earth as humans is truly humbling in comparison to heavenly beings and God themselves. Even in the Old Testament days of Enoch and others, the average lifespan of a person was roughly a mere few hundred years. In contrast, our Creator and heavenly entities such as angels and archangels have an undisclosed lifespan that seems unending or, at the very least, would last centuries and eons more than imaginable. In theory, this could mean that a plan of salvation or ideas of improvements needed to emerge good-doing beings from destruction will take time. Being left in the dark, no good-willed human would be able to fully prepare in all their strength for what is to come, and so the Lord stepped in to provide Enoch, one of their true and loyal followers, with visions that would eventually create a chain reaction towards rebuilding the good in humanity that was lost due to the Watchers' devious actions. Enoch himself may not live to see the undoing but became an important catalyst for those that would come after him.

Fortunately, Enoch's words to his family were taken with sincerity and trust, symbolizing the bond that he had with his sons, even as there were still decades of time to pass before action would be taken. In summarizing, Enoch's key points were on how the problem of the corruption of the earth by wicked men, fallen watchers, and Nephilim hybrids was to be resolved. As we know through Enoch and other biblical accounts, the world at this time was chaotic and violent, with the Nephilim desiring havoc-causing lifestyles and humans later on discovering works of metal crafting, creating weaponry, and armor. As it's shown, these struggles and painful experiences had only brought about more pain and suffering.

Finally, as the earth was reaching its breaking point, causing innocents to suffer along with the corrupt, the Lord devised and shared His plan with Enoch. Just as Enoch had wondered, the Lord was not unaware of these happenings and, furthermore, had created just the right processes to take care of the issue. First, Enoch experiences a vision of the beginnings of the hierarchy of heaven and most notably views the final resting place for human souls to return to once their time on earth was over. Additionally, those who were judged to be wicked would be sent to an endless void of suffering to compensate for their cruelty during their time living. Finally, as Enoch wondered what was to come of angels who fell from their grace and disobeyed the lord (in this case, the watchers descending to live as man does), he is shown a chasm-like prison where a similar negative experience awaited those angelic beings. Of course, like the prisoners in this category were considerably more powerful than the spirit of a human, angels were also seen standing guard at their posts to ensure the security of others.

Finally, just as the Lord had devised a plan for where to take sinful humans and angels alike, there was a call for a need to complete the physical requirements to rebalance life on earth. As Enoch had begun to understand, this would be done through a great natural disaster, more notably a flood that would swell across all of the corrupted lands and cleanse out hundreds of souls in preparation for their judgment. In order to complete this task successfully, God had determined that there must be one who is righteous enough to craft the equipment needed to survive the flood, not only for the sake of continuing the cycles of humanity but to ensure other walks of life would flourish after the passing of the Great Flood. To do so, Enoch had understood that the burden would lie upon his descendant Noah, who would be born as a visibly gifted individual, worthy of righteousness in his faith in the Lord.

With this, Enoch had understood what was still to come hundreds of years in the future, even after his time was completed, but also found relief in the fact that his lineage and predecessors' history would still flourish as this time went on. Naturally, he had explained all of these events to the best of his ability to his son Methuselah, who then documented them to keep in mind once the time had arrived. As one could imagine, this was of great relief when Methuselah and his own son Lamech were questioning the incidents or environments working to affect them as well. For example, at the time of Noah's birth, it was noted in the Book of Enoch that Noah was physically and spiritually distinguished among his peers, and as it was vastly different, there was an initial concern of angelic corruption or sinfulness that may have caused this change. Fortunately, Lamech and Methuselah were able to seek guidance from Enoch and further understand that they had misunderstood the intentions underlying Noah's individuality, explaining that it was not established to cause harm but to portray the young infant as one who will grow to do great things in the world. Of course, the latter explanation was shown to be accurate as an adult Noah would go on to both construct the ark and manage all who boarded it, man and beast.

One last major message that Enoch had desired to share with his family was one of the Son of Man, or the messiah himself. Although Enoch had envisioned the messiah through a metaphorical depiction of an animal sent to save other species from their own apocalypse, the message soon became clear on the requirements that the Righteous One would bring into the world. In this concept, the theme of mercy is shown at its greatest. As God had created the final destinations for both wicked and righteous souls to be placed, there were more greyscaled souls that would need further assessment. Through the messiah that was soon to come, many people were given the option of repentance for their sinful accounts. Naturally, this would mean that one's regret would need to be sincere as well, but as a blanket statement, this procedure would allow those who were remorseful or truly intended for good in the world to be fairly judged and placed. Of course, Enoch may not have known that after the flood, this would occur with the story and sacrifice of Jesus Christ, but the overall concept was introduced in order to show a more comprehensive view of the methods used in God's overall judgment and decisions.

The entirety of Enoch's visions may sound like a lot to take in at one time, but with the help of the synopses in this book, along with notable verses and real-life comparisons, the lessons should be easier to digest. There is also plenty of time to re-read sections and look up more details on an event too, as even Enoch's own family had to pace themselves with the knowledge brought forth in their lives by their ancestors. As with the emergence of the birth of Noah, this reference was especially as important as the reassurance it brought Lamech and Methuselah had supported the past words of Enoch and, by extension, the plan set in motion by the Lord. With this said, Enoch begins his final message.

Enoch begins his declaration by stating that all who had observed the Lord's rules and guidelines (simply put, the Ten Commandments) will need to wait for the time when those who work in evil would be destroyed and judged into their final destination. As per Enoch's understanding, the Lord plans to erase even the smallest mention of their corruptive existence from the Earth, which on the surface sounded like a tall work order for improvement. To understand this more, Enoch had the chance to see a vision involving a place only described as a blazing fire, feeling of pain and lamentation made for these fallen angels' wickedness against God and His creations, in addition to its non-angelic counterparts designated for human souls. In contrast, those who had followed the guidance and word of God through strife, distractions of worldly things such as riches and gold, and any passing challenge the Lord may give them would be further blessed with good fortune in all they do. With these final messages, Enoch had given the opportunity for Methuselah and his further descendants to continue to follow the Lord and trust in the process of what was still to come as the judgment was to pass through the world, giving due diligence towards wrongdoers and faithful spirits alike.

Today, similar concepts and ideas are explored in many of our everyday lives, as we must find our faith and endurance just as Enoch, Methuselah, and Lamech did. As people on earth, there are many concerns and questions that may erupt numerous times through life, whether it is a small choice in what to wear or eat or significant lifestyle changes such as the exploration of a new career path. Regardless, taking consolation from well-doing family and friends on where your next journey might take you is key to settling any feelings of uncertainty, as is thoughtful meditation or prayer. Additionally, the concept of final messages sent from one's predecessors is a theme in the Book of Enoch's final chapter as well, as the privilege to experience the final notes of an individual or family member who had overcome their own struggles is not always a right in these times, but the knowledge one may want to share at their end can oftentimes be priceless towards the receiver. Overall, just as Enoch's family had become concerned with the emergence of something new when faced with their own struggles and corruption in their world, both the Lord's guidance and righteous peers allow one time to deconstruct any concern and continue to move forward into progress and ideally, a better world.

CHAPTER EIGHT:

A Gathering of Heavenly Beings

Chapter Eight:

A Gathering of Heavenly Beings

Throughout the Book of Enoch, there are many references to gatherings of numerous types of heavenly beings, either experienced directly by Enoch through his spiritual journey into the many layers of heaven or through retellings of how the Watchers and other angels had strayed from their true path. At the beginning of Enoch's journey, a simple depiction of heaven is shown with simple, earthly processes being monitored. Similar to a control room or simply depicted stereotypes of angelic beings living in clouds and controlling the weather, this is where Enoch had his first experience with seeing heavenly beings at work.

In contrast to this first image of the foundation that heaven worked upon, in the next level of heaven, Enoch had seen an image contrasting to the first; a prison keeping corrupt and traitorous angels in line. Although these heavenly beings were once part of the inner workings of heaven themselves, their actions and blatant decisions to turn away from God or interfere in human affairs (such as the Watchers themselves had), they were now considered rebellious, destructive, and unfit to their duties. This is a great example of how even the Lord's most loyal could be coaxed into temptations by evil beings and implies the further solution of judgment to be necessary in order to bring balance back to all humans on earth.

Next, Enoch had come to see a vision of the contrast between an angelic guarded Garden of Eden and the abyss of emptiness and torture that awaits cruel and malicious human beings. At its most basic, this refers to the contrasting ideas of Heaven and Hell or a place of paradise for the true and endless suffering of wrongdoers. Moving further into the fourth section of heaven and heading further towards God were the details and workings of celestial bodies, most importantly the Sun and Moon. Moving around the sun, a few more heavenly beings were noticed; Chalkydri and phoenixes. Similar to the ancient Greek depiction of what a phoenix would look like, Enoch's vision of heaven's phoenixes has implied a similar look, as they are described as flying and dwelling alongside the Sun, assisting in the comings and goings of daylight on Earth. Chalkydri, another angelic species, are also notably flying with the phoenix, alerting birds to the beginning of daybreak with song. To carry on this chorus of introducing the new morning, a group of angels was also noted singing in harmony.

In the following fifth and sixth levels of heaven, Enoch had witnessed the archangels and Watchers themselves. With his approach, Enoch had the opportunity to discuss with the fallen Watchers, or Grigori, as they were now referred to, due to their loyalty to Satan for their wrongdoings against the Lord. With these discussions, Enoch had successfully encouraged some of the Grigori to repent as they lay in limbo awaiting their judgment. When viewing the activities of the Archangels in the sixth level, Enoch was able to see all that they had managed on heaven and earth in the Lord's name. Everything from assigning tasks to lower-level angels to ensuring the natural balance is in order for humans below had been tasked to the Archangels, making them hold more responsibility overall. Here, leaving the sixth level and entering the seventh, Enoch had the chance to meet Gabriel, who then became his guide for the remainder of his visions of heaven.

With these depictions, it is easy to see the varying needs that the Lord must fulfill and establish through the heavens. Similar today to an average office, there is a diversified variety of types of beings who are all specialized and accurate in the positions they hold. For example, you may have your everyday workers, managers, and individuals with certain expertise, but in order for everything to work together, each holds a significant weight of responsibility to keep things running smoothly. According to Enoch's visions, every angelic being had their own authority to help 'run the business' of heaven. From the common angels to celestial beasts, to even the Archangels who held the majority of responsibility for the others had their own purpose created for them. With this understanding, the decisions of the watchers' corruption and betrayal to reside with humans appear even more dire and disruptive to all who were on heaven and earth. Fortunately, with the loyalty of the Lord's Archangels, Enoch was recruited to share the information on what was soon to come and how the earth would be replenished after the events restoring it would pass.

As Gabriel joins Enoch, the two finally meet the near-conclusion of their journey, coming ever so closer to the residing place of the Lord Himself. At this point, Enoch is able to catch a glimpse of God and what looks to be a throne from a distance away, but the time to see Him up close hasn't arrived quite yet. The seventh level of heaven can be depicted as similar to the living area of all angelic beings. Filled with archangels, angels, and seraphim alike, the imagery shown to Enoch was almost too much to handle from a human's perspective. Emerging into this light-filled residence of all angels, Enoch is greeted by Michael, who further reassures and strengthens Enoch's senses to prepare him to continue on his journey. Finally, Enoch reaches the farthest layer of the inner workings of heaven, through the eighth and ninth layers of celestial constellations to God Himself. Here, Enoch is anointed by Michael and blessed in preparation to finalize his soul, likewise that of the angels. As previously mentioned, this is the beginning of a cloudier understanding of how Enoch has been accepted and finally ascended into heaven. In simple terms, this anointing causes a separation of Enoch's soul and earthly body, ensuring that within a limited amount of time, Enoch will ascend back to heaven from the earth to spend eternity with God once he had spread the word and final instructions of what is still to come to his son Methuselah.

CHAPTER NINE:

The Fallen and the War That Never Ends

Chapter Nine:

The Fallen and the War That Never Ends

The visions that Enoch had the opportunity to see on the beginnings and solutions of so much sin and corruption on Earth is a commonly repeated story. In Enoch's case, this is shown in the decisions of the Watchers to decide to live amongst humans, take their own wives, and create their own offspring, all of which would defy the will of God. According to this tale, angels and humans weren't meant to mix and procreate by design, as they lived in very different circumstances and were given vastly different guidelines on their duties. By ignoring this keystone rule, these angels who were meant to be in a position of monitoring life on the Earth were deemed turned from or fallen from God as they attempted to live as a human would. To make matters worse, their offspring were described as beings completely lacking in harmony and balance. Depicted as giants, these Nephilim were said to be chaotic, unruly, and a danger to humanity. According to Enoch's visions, the Nephilim were essentially Waging War against humans and even resorting to heinous acts such as eating them. Overall, the falling of the Watchers and the chaos that grew from it disrupted the fragile balance that the world and humanity depended on.

In modern retellings, this plot can be found not only in text-based religious adaptations such as the story of Noah's ark but in many other tales of major betrayals. One exceptional example of this in storytelling can be found in many of Shakespeare's works. In many of his tales, there are elements of shock as betrayals occur among opposing political forces, birth lineages, and even within families. In contrast, many of Shakespeare's works end in tragedy for his characters, but the presence of similar themes he explores leaves it to wonder if he had taken inspiration from biblical tales, including the one of Enoch and his family.

Finally, Enoch learns of the only way to stop this chaos and rebalance the Earth for humanity. To do so, God must create a series of times of judgment for the watchers and their offspring, all while simultaneously cleansing the earth of the horrendous marks the two groups had left in their paths. In this circumstance, a great flood was to be called for, along with an eventual rebirth of all that is good through Enoch's eventual descendants (later understood to be Noah and his family) and the animal species that are meant to accompany them. Afterward and centuries down the line, one final day of judgment for all people of the earth will be called for as well in order to ensure balance and prosperity for those who chose to do good and pain for those who became influenced by the corrupt former watchers and acted likewise. Until that final time, it may seem as though heaven and earth are constricted into a constant state of war without an end nearby unless faith is felt in the meantime.

Imagine your favorite novel, movie, or video game; was there ever a time when the 'good guys' came face to face with a conflict so big that it seemed impossible to overcome? In many stories, especially in genres based on action or adventure, the main character often finds themselves faced with unbeatable odds or a disaster caused by an antagonist with no end in sight. This imbalance of their world would typically paint a bleak ending, but due to the hero's faith and perseverance in good overcoming evil, there is always a way to restore balance, save the world, and win their war that never ends.

Enoch's visions and hope for the future mirror these themes of patience and faith. Nearly all of the premonitions that Enoch has the opportunity to see and share with his family later on, are summarized into a condensed version of what is to come, and in reality, the actual events may take years to emerge. Additionally, as Enoch has nearly completed his own experience and life on earth, it's likely to assume that these events won't even affect Enoch himself directly, making his faith in these visions coming to fruition that much more remarkable. This really shows how dependable Enoch had been as a recipient of these visions and a messenger to later generations!

Just before Enoch had passed, Noah was said to be born with the appearance of an extraordinary child, but it wouldn't be until long after Enoch had ascended to the Lord that Noah's blessings would finally be revealed and put to use. As previously compared, this also emphasizes the idea that time in relation to the way we keep track of it from a human point of view is not synonymous with the time being kept by the angels and God. There are essentially decades of time spent from the birth of Noah to the peak of Noah's importance through building the ark. Considering the modern sense of keeping time, one human life is simply a blip in the span of the centuries and eons covered from the earth's creation to its' final day of judgment. With this all in mind, it's easier to see how the lord may have created these eras of judgment, such as the great flood, to reflect a more expansive timeline. It proves to show that although these events seem to have taken their time to be completed, they were most likely right on schedule from a heavenly standpoint. Overall, this further emphasizes the need for faith in our own lives and purpose, that regardless of our own small-scale experiences, there very well be a bigger picture behind the scenes that is yet to come in order to ensure activities done through good intentions to be praised and wrongdoings condemned. At times it may seem like your own eternal war is continuing to wage, but do not falter and keep the faith! There will always be a chance for life to come back into balance…it may just be a bit longer than anticipated.

CHAPTER TEN:

THE MESSIAH AS SEEN IN ENOCH

CHAPTER TEN:

THE MESSIAH AS SEEN IN ENOCH

As Enoch had experienced a plethora of intriguing visions of importance, one, in particular, holds the Book of Enoch into the category of notoriety as a key detail; the emergence and eventual coming of the Messiah himself. Shown in the Parables section of Enoch's story and journey through heaven, Enoch receives a significant vision of the coming of the Messiah, Jesus Christ. At this point, he is not yet named but referred to as the Son of Man, or Righteous One, but through Enoch's narrative, we are able to understand the importance of his interactions with people centuries down the line. According to Enoch, the messiah was envisioned seated on a throne of glory, similar to the throne the Lord had dwelled upon and would have the main task of salvation for those who had rejected God through the judgment of their actions.

Although Enoch distinctly depicts a savior or messiah that heavily alludes to the eventual coming of Jesus hundreds of years ahead of Enoch's time, it isn't without controversy. As one begins their journey through approaching this text, the tellings of Enoch may even come as a surprise, as they are only briefly referenced in modern biblical texts or brushed over in many religious reference books. Many even contest the creation of the book itself, as discoveries have shown copies of the Book of Enoch close to a few centuries before the age of Christ. In support, there is also a significant level of evidence that supports the legitimacy of Enoch's tellings, as there have been scripture sections of the Book of Enoch depicted on the Dead Sea Scrolls (believed to have been constructed as early as three centuries before Christ), as well a referenced by biblical figures that lived after Enoch's time, including Jesus himself.

Ironically, one of the most controversial aspects of the Book of Enoch also revolves around Jesus as well. First discovered as the Son of Man and later as humanity's messiah through Enoch's visions, the references and descriptions of how the Lord would guide his Son and what miracles of salvation would emerge from his actions are explained fairly accurately. In our modern times, this brings concern and confusion as some may doubt the knowledge Enoch had received as a whole. In addition to this, another argument against Enoch is with the existence of Jesus himself, meaning that the confirmation of the existence of the Messiah before his actual introduction is not a legitimate scenario and wouldn't fit with the rest of biblical scripture.

Regardless of these concerns, many others who are interested in further studies of biblical accounts or historical tales, in general, have analyzed and translated the Book of Enoch for others to understand and determine for themselves what truths there are to find in his accounts. In terms of the Book of Enoch's legitimacy, there is also one final concept that must be considered and has been covered in these past chapters, and that is the concept of time in regards to heavenly beings. To reiterate, the events and chronology of the Lord's plans or the activities of angelic beings may not be tracked accurately with our modern understanding of time. As God Himself is older than the documentation or even concept of time, it is not unreasonable for Them to bypass the laws of time in their oversight of human activities on Earth. Reasonably so, this would mean that if the Lord had intended to bring a messiah upon Earth to bring salvation to sinful souls, He could just as easily tease this preview of what is to come to an individual as loyal as Enoch. Despite the limited knowledge of some concepts that we may not have yet uncovered, the Book of Enoch holds a significant number of lessons to be learned regardless of individual perspectives.

Further indicating the continued importance of the emergence of the Messiah, Enoch reveals that there will soon be a time when the Son of God will descend onto earth to live among the righteous and sinners alike, further-reaching towards the humanitarian cause of repentance and loyalty towards God. As the image of the Messiah continues his journey, Enoch notes that even the greatest, most powerful kings and rulers will be humbled before him (a foreshadowing of the intense following and loyalty the Messiah will withhold over both common folk and leaders of rich lands), and would further have the strength to symbolically strike them down from their power or entitlement if their goals are those against the Lord, or are sinful in nature. Overall, the messiah would embody hope through their intentions of relieving the world of darkness and sinful deeds enacted by others, creating light in their darkness, and a sense of salvation towards those who turn into the light for repentance—in the end, leaving an era of peace for all who remained true and just in their intentions.

In some translations of the Book of Enoch, there may be some confusion on the depiction of the Messiah, as slight word changes may lead the reader to imply that Enoch himself was shown to be the Son of Man and, by extension, God. Regardless of this confusion, this is not the case, and the general consensus is that Enoch does not see a depiction of himself in these visions. Around the end of the Parables section, Enoch is shown to continue his journey into heaven, and by the time he had finally reached the residing areas of the archangels and God at the final levels, Enoch is greeted comfortably as 'that Son of Man,' born of righteousness.

Again, among many scholars or researchers, there are likely theories that a necessary passage belonging to the Book of Enoch has yet to be found, which may have the chance to clear up this language (and later confusion) still hasn't been found, so in the most likely scenario, it is suggested that in order not to contradict the tellings of the New Testament, that in this situation, Enoch being referred to as the Son of Man, actually to translate into a more loosely based title. Enoch is indeed a righteous Son of Man, or one worthy enough to receive these visions and secrets of the inner-workings of heaven, but is not the exact individual that is being referred to as chosen to seat themselves on a throne with God and judge the happenings of the Earth. This may be the most accurate of all theories regarding the text and context of Enoch's story, yet may still be debatable among researchers and belief systems for the time being. Regardless of any possible translation errors, the visions Enoch received about the actions that will be taken by the Messiah had been deemed important for the Book of Enoch as a whole, as the depictions of judgment would play a part in the larger concept of God's plan to rid the earth of the recent corruption laid out from the Watchers and their children, in addition to the eventual (and inevitable due to the fallen's interruption) continuation of the wickedness and corruption acted upon by humans themselves, yet having mercy upon those who may sincerely regret their actions and work to repent their deeds.

CHAPTER ELEVEN:

Heavenly Wrath, Mercy, and Salvation

CHAPTER ELEVEN:

HEAVENLY WRATH, MERCY, AND SALVATION

Throughout the Book of Enoch, there are numerous examples of heavenly wrath, mercy, and salvation that are seen through Enoch's visions or, more intimately, through the documentation we have on the future deeds of his descendant, Noah. Beginning with the betrayal of the Watchers, who were meant to only monitor humans on earth, we see the ways the Lord is able to resolve this issue. From Gabriel's assignment leading to many of the Watchers' children to wage their wars and chaos upon each other to the final destinations of where their wickedness would be jailed away forever, there are a diverse set of options that seem to await those who rejected the Lord terrifyingly!

Although the Archangel Gabriel's work alone was efficient in clearing some of the chaos away from innocent human bystanders and redirecting it towards other Nephilim, the situation as a whole would still leave room for improvement. Later on, this concern would be solved by the Great Flood. As the Lord provided Enoch with the information of how these events would eventually come to fruition, He later began preparing Noah for the physical act of saving numerous species and carrying on his own lineage through building the Ark as the Lord began the creation of a Great Flood to immerse these Nephilim and whisk them away towards their inevitable judgment for their deeds. In addition, it is safe to say that many cruel personalities worn on some of the humans living in this time were also carried away to their judgment, as the purpose of the Flood was to cleanse the sins of a corrupted world, only leaving a balanced form of nature in its absence.

Once the watchers, Nephilim, and humans were collected for their time of judgment, Enoch had noted several options for their consequence. First, for many deceitful or ill-turned angels, there laid a prison of sorts connected to the lowest levels of heaven. Likewise, an area similar to the one suited for fallen heavenly beings was deemed fit for corrupt, sinful human beings to stay for eternity.

Here, these people or angels were sent to be consumed in fire, pain, and torture, creating punishments for acts irredeemable and non-regrettable for those fallen angels. For those such as the Nephilim, a type of purgatory was mentioned as a form of punishment similar to the angelic prisons. Instead of images of pain and traditional punishment that might come to mind, the cruel Nephilim's fate was described as the lack of much of anything. Depicted as barren, cold, and empty, a Tartarus-like void was designated for these corrupt beings, which arguably might even be a fate worse than the ones met by fallen angels or humans.

Throughout all of Enoch's visions of what was to be for the deceitful and untrue, it is clear to see that despite all the goodness and well-made intentions established by the Lord are prolific, final judgments and deeds are withheld to the utmost importance when it came to betrayal, or wickedness, further displaying how essential a true balance of even the overall goodness of heaven must be held carefully.

Just as there are consequences for poor actions, there is still mercy and redemption displayed through Enoch's visions of heaven. One of the first glimpses of this phenomenon occurs within Enoch's journey through the layers of heaven. As he gets the chance to meet some angels who decided to deflect away from the Lord and instead follow the guidance of Satan, Enoch recalls being able to deter them from their previous betrayals and seek forgiveness. Surprisingly, a few who were still awaiting their turn in judgment genuinely did just that and were eventually redeemed from their sins. Later on, Enoch would learn of the righteous actions that would take place later on in the age of the Messiah on Earth, which is fully documented throughout the New Testament. In the latter case, Jesus himself becomes both a literal and metaphorical symbol of offering mercy and redemption regardless of the outward appearance and thoughts that those individuals may not look as though they were worthy of saving.

Finally, the Lord shows the entirety of the meaning of salvation and mercy through the struggles humans would have to endure throughout the catastrophe the Nephilim and Watchers had brought through His method of cleansing the land. With the assistance of Noah, the Lord had the opportunity and all the pieces to collect those who didn't deserve the punishment of great flooding and were selected to continue acts of goodness long after the floods had been completed. Later, as people had begun corrupting the world and influencing others to follow their lead, the Messiah was brought to encourage them to repent instead of facing dire consequences for their actions. Last but not least, when the final implied coming of judgment is upon the world again, as per Enoch's final visions, there will be one last round of potential redemption for those who genuinely desire to reject their previous desires to wreak havoc or cause pain to others.

Despite Enoch's recollection of the variations of heavenly wrath that are available for both angelic and earthly beings alike, the goal of God's plans is not to cause fear but to exemplify themes of justice and equality. Contrasted to our modern forms of court, punishment, and judgment, nowhere in Enoch's journey does he mention any instance of beings wrongfully judged in the eyes of the Lord (or later, as the Son of God is alluded to managing the need of judgment on spirits), further implying that God is truly all-knowing regarding one's true intentions and desires.

As a general understanding when it comes to judgment, He is all-knowing and able to diagnose where to assign each soul or being that properly approaches Him. In comparison to life on earth, today we are aware that some personalities get through their lives by acting deceitful, cunning, or competitive to the point of fault in selfishness, and may even get away with it for years, flaunting success where it is not earned while the earnest of us are left behind. Despite this, at the end of their time on earth, there will soon be a time of judgment, where the Lord will weigh their actions upon the world and amongst their peers to find their true belonging, resting in paradise or suffering in the darkness.

Although they may differ in the details, many other religious texts offer their interpretation of similar concepts as Enoch had experienced, including the concept of karma, which could be applied to the people of the times of the Old Testament. Generally speaking, karma is a Buddhist and Hindu theory that people will eventually get what they deserve in terms of their good and bad actions. This means that if a person performs mostly evil deeds, their karma or results of their life will be negative. In itself, it can be easy to argue that karma is not an entirely encompassing view of the methods God uses to place His final judgment but combined with the salvation brought by Jesus and the analysis of one's true intentions or desire to repent for their cruel actions, it is not hard to see how even in the final stages of judgment, the Lord has a well thought out, accurate plan for all.

CHAPTER TWELVE:

THE ENDURING

CHAPTER TWELVE:

THE ENDURING

Along with metaphorical or literal usages of faith and loyalty that the Book of Enoch explores, there is a sense of enduring throughout Enoch's spiritual journey as well. Based on the dictionary, enduring, or endurance, is defined as a continuous action or something that is relatively long-lasting in nature. Although in some cases, enduring and faith may be used interchangeably, some may consider the term 'faith' as one that is situational. For example, if you're on a long road trip and your vehicle starts to act unsteady, you might have to put faith in your situation that there will be a rest stop where you are able to diagnose the issue.

Many challenges in life require faith, either in physical outcomes or by a message directly from the Lord Himself. With this modern viewpoint, having faith may seem like more of a fleeting emotion or temporary state of mind. Considering this point of view, faith might not seem to be an enduring quality for some, although it objectively should be.

Enduring, on the other hand, signifies a steady and consistent outlook on life. Runners competing in an endurance race are not judged directly on their speed but on their ability to reach far distances that an average person would be exhausted by within minutes. Enduring involves many other traits to successfully achieve a goal as well, such as perseverance, innovation, and even faith itself. When pushed to extreme limits, it is nearly unbelievable how much the average human body can endure.

As far back as the beginnings of civilization, many tribes are evidenced to show tremendous feats of endurance through harsh cold, heat, and scarcity in resources. Today, feats of endurance are still being shown in regard to the human body through world records and personal achievements. Continuing the example of marathoners, one of the longest marathons in the world, the Self-Transcendence Race in Jamaica consists of 3,100 miles (or 4989 km) that is covered by runners in approximately 52 days with only six hours to rest and replenish their calorie preserves.

In order to successfully complete this challenge, runners must have an extraordinary sense of endurance, both mentally and physically, to reach their goals, and despite all odds, many have successfully completed this great challenge.

Although the guidelines are fairly simple in themselves, the concept of running over twelve hours in a day repetitively would be an exhausting feat, but just as Enoch and his family had endured the challenges that were brought to their lives concerning the watchers and eventual Great Flood, the runners must put their faith in what is still to come, envisioning that finish line and eventual feeling of overwhelming accomplishment in achieving their goals. In Enoch's case, this means to look not only at what challenges were in front of him but the ones that have yet to cross his (or, by extension, his family's) path.

Overall, the faith and resilience in the plans of the Lord that were still left to be carried out gave hope to those to who Enoch had left his tales, which was much needed later on as the world became more corrupt and Noah set out to build the Ark to preserve both humans and animals alike.

Through the Book of Enoch, we see Enoch enduring through the visions he is able to receive, no matter how complex they may seem to be at first. As he took his journey through the levels of heaven to reach God's throne, Enoch bore witness to numerous scenes from the jailed punishments awaiting fallen angels to the heavenly beings said to control, monitor, and guide celestial bodies as important as the sun. With this in mind, it's easy to imagine how visually overloading imagery like this may be for a person born on the earth to witness for the first time and spurs the question of how many would abandon their position in exchange for fewer complications to endure. Would you be of strong mind and spirit to bear the truths Enoch had gained responsibility for?

It would be difficult for any one of us to tell, but fortunately, Enoch had just the right balance of both to continue and support the will of God. His wisdom of over three hundred years' life experience before ascending to heaven, his righteousness, and presumably many other characteristics we may not have all the knowledge of had allowed Enoch first to endure these visions and later endure the tasks of reassuring his family of the blessings their child Noah would bring upon the earth, as well as the plan already set in action to rid the world of the corruptions that the Watchers, Nephilim, and cruel people of the earth had set in motion to change the natural balance of life.

Overall, enduring individuals such as Enoch, Methuselah, and later Noah are celebrated for their perseverance and near-constant faith (near-constant is mentioned in this case as no one human can be perfect, and by nature, we all arguably struggle with our faith at one point or another) throughout their time on Earth. Just as God acts steady with intention and endurance, so should the followers of the Lord.

When the will to endure is found to be lacking, it is important to note that external influences can rejuvenate this trait as well? As Methuselah had noticed their child bearing an infant Noah so remarkably different than before with powerful energy surrounding them, their first reaction was one of shock and concern. Of all things, Methuselah was most likely cautious of what the meaning of this extraordinary child would come to be.

Fortunately, Methuselah decided to pursue the knowledge and past visions of Enoch, and after learning of the circumstances, Enoch had the ability to strongly reassure Methuselah that Noah's distinct differences were not a curse or any sign of negativity at all. On the contrary, Noah would be destined to contribute a great deal towards both heaven and humanity as a whole through their actions as an adult. In turn, this reassured Methuselah that not only would their grandchild eventually do great things but that their entire family lineage was ensured to be in good hands as the Lord promised.

Finally, just as Enoch had mentioned, Noah would find himself in his own situation of enduring his faith through the struggles of creating a vessel fit for a plethora of animal species and his own extended family to reside in during the events of the Great Flood. The impact of approximately forty days and nights at sea in itself would also become another challenge of endurance.

As time grows longer, the chances of becoming impatient and increases of doubts may occur. Despite all of the challenges, it is clear to see that the determination, perseverance, and enduring of all of these biblical figures had paid off in the end, as their loyalty and desire to do good by the Lord had outweighed any fears or doubts that He would not keep his word at bay, even when they themselves might not live on earth long enough to witness the conclusion of His plan.

CHAPTER THIRTEEN:

ENOCH STILL SPEAKS TO US TODAY

Chapter Thirteen:

Enoch Still Speaks to Us Today

Many of the visions and messages that Enoch had experienced many years ago can still be applied to modern life in the 21st century. One of the largest blanketing themes of the journeys Enoch had experienced is the involvement of heaven in the evaluation of all life on earth. Similar to any other record-keeping (albeit much more intimate and personalized), Enoch notes that there are hundreds of angels and heavenly beings that work behind the scenes to ensure God's wills are carried out properly each and every day.

Additionally, there are many lessons to be learned along the way of Enoch's journey, from the understanding of the emergence and spread of sin to the opportunity to repent for those wrongdoings if genuinely desired. Regardless of our choices and decisions, it is clear that even today, the temptation exists in many forms for all of us, further signifying the need for spiritual strengthening and exercising in the ways of the Lord despite how well-versed one may be. One small action has the potential to create huge waves in the process of cause and effect, so it is essential to understand the underlying reasoning as to why a situation may be tempting in its own right. As humans living in the lifestyles that we must, we are prone to slipping up every now and again, but the intentions and desire to do good are what truly matter in the eyes of the lord come the time of judgment.

Naturally, there are interferences among the ideals of the Lord that had been brought upon by Satan, as well as the empty promises of rewards through wickedness as well. One major example of this interruption would be the decision of the Watchers to abandon their positions in order to take their own human wives and attempt to live on Earth. As a result, their children, the Nephilim, emerge as beings of chaos and destruction, increasing conflict among all else on Earth. As with other aspects of His all-knowing vision, the Lord has a plan to resolve this conflict and restore the balance of life on Earth. As Gabriel the Archangel begins the task to redirect the Nephilim and wicked tribes of men unto each other in terms of their endlessly waged war, the Lord was preparing for a Great Flood of judgment for the cruel souls residing among those who were true.

In order to complete His plans, God reached out to Enoch. A man descended from Adam through seven generations, deemed with a righteous and loyal mindset who would experience specific visions regarding the changes brought into both heaven and earth to re-establish a prolific place for all who are worthy of it. With this, Enoch had the ability to reassure his own children and grandchildren of the path they would have yet to take, giving meaning to the bigger picture of salvation the entirety of humanity would face.

Just as Enoch had, there may have been times in your own life where fear of change of the unknown has affected your decisions. Whether it's a move to a new place, changing careers, or even more sudden changes that would affect daily routine, these changes can seem uncertain enough for life to feel as though they just stopped. In most cases, life will still go on, so what is one to do? For example, during a wave of sudden layoffs, one might be initially shocked or blindsided at the outcome. Next, as the information processes, thoughts may be racing on what should be next to come, and making a plan would be essential.

Similar to the stories of Enoch, this sudden change in life would be concerning and even distressing without faith in the good yet to come. Enoch's world was strife with chaos as the Watchers, and their offspring were set out to destroy it, making life and survival full of plenty of what-ifs. Despite these struggles, Enoch had persevered in his desire to continue to live a good life and eventually had received divine information that the end of all pain and suffering for those on earth, as well as the punishments earned by wickedness, were still to come. With this knowledge, even at the ending of his own time on Earth, Enoch had the opportunity to reassure his son Methuselah and grandson on the fate of their family later on by reassuring him that Noah's stark unique features and composition would help bring them closer to God and become the vessel for preserving life on earth.

With these tales in mind, it is reassuring that no matter how disorienting modern life may be when faced with a new challenge, by leaning into good intentions and your own intuition, there may be an even better opportunity that awaits your future. The Lord Himself takes time to bring plans to fruition, so do not be discouraged in waiting for results or even seeing your own goals in completion, as the very best is still to come through slow, consistent change and improvements. In the case of the Book of Enoch, the span between the falling of the Watchers, the pleading of the Archangels to repair their former allies' damages to the Earth, and even the interactions of Enoch himself had taken not years but generations of living in order to become a drawn-out and successful procedure fully. By the time the final act of God had been set in motion, Enoch would be already at his rest in heaven, leaving his great-grandchild Noah, now a wizened adult in his own right, to proceed with God's will through building the Ark. Regardless, Enoch had acted as those who were righteous in their following of the Lord and transcribed all that he had envisioned in order to tell his family of what will await them as the years passed.

Even in the darkest of times, there is still light and hope, and as the Lord has shown through the visions and learnings of Enoch, there is always a larger plan that may be working itself out in the background; we may not be able to see around the corner quite yet.

Bibliography

Blum, J. (2018). The book of Enoch (2) The Sin of The Watchers. Retrieved Feb 14, 2022, https://blog.israelbiblicalstudies.com/jewish-studies/the-book-of-enoch-2-the-sin-of-the-watchers/

Charles, R. (1917). The book of Enoch. Retrieved Feb 14, 2022, https://www.sacred-texts.com/bib/boe/index.htm

Heartdweller, N. (2018). The Book of Enoch. Retrieved Feb 14, 2022, https://www.wattpad.com/416116441-book-of-enoch-section-i-chapters-1-36

Laurence, R. (1883). The Book of Enoch. Retrieved Feb 14, 2022, https://www.sacred-texts.com/bib/bep/bep02.htm

The watchers in The Book of Enoch - the angels who betrayed God, explained. (2022). Feb 14, 2022, https://mythologyexplained.com/the-watchers-in-the-book-of-enoch/

Williams, J. The Apocrypha and Pseudepigrapha of the Old Testament BOOK OF ENOCH. (1995). Retrieved Feb 14, 2022, https://www.ccel.org/c/charles/otpseudepig/enoch/ENOCH_1.HTM

De Young, S. (2020). The Book of Enoch. Retrieved Feb 14, 2022, https://blogs.ancientfaith.com/wholecounsel/2020/07/25/the-book-of-enoch/

Authors

J. Blum - The book of Enoch (2) The Sin of The Watchers (2018)

R.H. Charles - The Book of Enoch (1917)

Ni Heartdweller - The Book of Enoch (2018)

R. Laurence - The Book of Enoch (1883)

Mythology Explained (blog, no author) - The angels who Betrayed God, Explained

J. Williams - The Apocrypha and Pseudepigrapha of the Old Testament (1995)

Friar. S. De Young - The Book of Enoch (2020)